THE FOREBODING

THE FOREBODING

M.J. FOLEY

NEW DEGREE PRESS

COPYRIGHT © 2023 M.J. FOLEY

THE FOREBODING

ISBN   979-8-88926-912-0 *Paperback*

         979-8-88926-805-5 *Hardcover*

         979-8-88926-913-7 *Ebook*

To the women who want to be more and do it all.

"Until you realize how easy it is for your
mind to be manipulated, you remain the
puppet of someone else's game."

—EVITA OCHEL

AUTHOR'S NOTE

Most people believe we as humans only use ten percent of our brains, but this is simply not true. Almost all of our brain is in use all the time. The human body and the human mind are extraordinarily complex, and the sheer volume of tasks occurring subconsciously and simultaneously just to maintain baseline functionality is mind numbing, all puns intended. In fact, according to Dr. John Henley, a neurologist at the Mayo Clinic, as well as numerous research publications across scientific journals, humans use one hundred percent of the brain throughout the course of a day. Even while asleep, some regions of the brain such as the frontal cortex or the somatosensory areas remain active (Boyd 2008).

We also tend to believe that humans are special and different from other life on Earth. We think of ourselves as superior in intelligence, dominant over all other life forms. We have started ignoring the interconnectedness of humans and other living beings that used to be vital for survival.

Instead, we prop ourselves up with technology and invest our research dollars and intellectual capital into ensuring we inorganically maintain dominance. Whether it be through powerful weaponry, expansion of human presence into new frontiers, or simply longer lifespans, we aim to elongate and maximize time here on Earth at any cost.

As a lover of nature and novels and a degree-holder in cognitive science, technical writing, and engineering, I have developed many conflicting feelings and questions about the world we live in. Where is our place? Where should we be researching and investing our precious time and energy?

The weak, but ever-present electromagnetic current coursing through all living things, big or small, fascinates me but has rarely been brought to life in fiction.

In humans, this current thrums in the form of electric nerve impulses. Well-established technology in the medical world, for example deep brain stimulators and pacemakers, tap into those electric nerve impulses and supplement them. These devices have resulted in astounding improvements for those whose bodies would have otherwise failed. You may be aware of or even have experienced these advanced treatments.

The world of cognitive neuroscience also taps into those same currents to bolster the human connection. Technological advances are allowing people to "speak" and command each other's actions through direct brain-to-brain communication.

In fact, the US Defense Advanced Research Projects Agency (DARPA) gained approval for over five hundred implantations of deep brain electrodes capable of human-to-human thought transfer, with success rates of eighty-five percent. This success rate holds true even for people on opposite sides of the globe (Rio Times 2022). Many lay circles would declare this feat impossible if asked. However, technological facilitation has opened many doors to explore the mind's capabilities when channeling energy in just the right way.

The irony of technology as both a barrier and a catalyst to life's interconnectedness is not lost on me. Clearly, we are vested in our own human potential in a variety of applications. Why have we not been just as invested in understanding this power in other living organisms? Why is interconnectedness of nature's energy so often dismissed as naturalist propaganda?

For example, in his book *The Heartbeat of Trees*, Peter Wohlleben presents compelling evidence that trees feel, breathe, and might even have tiny brain-like structures in the tips of their roots. Yet he also reveals his career-long struggle in getting serious buy-in to explore and understand these phenomena (Wohlleben 2021).

His scientific explanations made me wonder, what would happen if we truly sought out organic connection with both each other and nature? Just think how the world might change if the complexity of humans and the vastness of nature joined together to hear and respond to each other's needs.

Maybe we don't have to be as independent as we think.

The Foreboding strives to explore the push and pull of such a power and the implications of a deeper connection coupled with the universal struggle of good versus evil that continues to define the human condition. Though this story and some of the concepts in it are fictional, they are not too far in the distant future. If you enjoy an imaginative story, suspenseful action, and thought-provoking natural science fiction, this novel is for you. I hope this book gives you a chance to think about what's possible, step outside your comfort zone, and, just for a while, open your mind to scientific, fantastic possibility.

CHAPTER 1

Peering sheepishly into the rearview mirror, Shiloh sighed, shaking her head in disbelief. How had she acquired this much stuff? She had always thought of herself as practical, but this move had proven to her that, if nothing else, she had an overstated version of practical.

At the most basic level, she left for the same reason most anybody did—to start fresh. She had toyed with the idea of picking up and starting over many times throughout the past few years but hadn't thought she'd have the fortitude to make up her mind and commit. Until now.

So while Joe traveled on yet another business trip, she had put all the major US cities she could think of in a hat and picked one. Two days later, before she had a chance to talk herself out of it, she packed up all her things into the biggest trailer she could manage and set off for Denver. The methodology had been so recklessly out-of-character that she had fallen in love with the spontaneity of it. By the time Joe noticed her absence, she was already two states away and ignoring every call.

On paper she knew she'd had it all, but something had gone missing somewhere along the way. The connection between her heart and her mind somehow broken. Numbness washed through her very core. Tired, anxious thoughts about should haves and could haves plagued her at night.

This state of turmoil had grown into a black hole in her stomach over the past few years and she couldn't handle it. A small part of her felt pulled in every direction, but instead of choosing one, she'd fallen into the paralyzing state of doing nothing. This would be different.

She took her time, stopping and enjoying her road trip and the oddities of the Midwest. At times she fell into tourist traps, but her favorite was finding the places only locals knew about. Her pale complexion, plain brown hair, and simple style helped her slip into these environments, blending with the landscape. She wouldn't want to stick out.

Instead of panicking with no plan and no income, Shiloh felt physically lighter the further she got from Pennsylvania. She could have sworn five pounds fell off her medium frame every time she entered a new state. She floated contentedly through this transient lifestyle, springing out of bed in the morning to explore each stop. Walks to coffee shops followed aimless, ambling conversations with pleasant souls exercising their dogs. At times their kindness felt so foreign it was easy to pretend she had been transported to another world.

When she arrived in Denver, she had been on the road for a little over two weeks but managed to secure herself a six-month lease in her new city. The place seemed to be in a relatively respectable part of town given her modest budget.

She hadn't found a job yet. However, she did have a nice nest egg built up. Her boring, albeit well-paying, physical science research assistant role had robbed her of most of her time since graduation five years ago, which made saving easy.

She didn't need a lot and didn't spend much, she reminded herself as anxiety started to creep into her thoughts.

As she pulled into the parking lot, her new residence welcomed her in a vaguely underwhelming way. The narrow one-way street, lined with loading docks for various industrial-looking warehouses, taunted her as she peered right and then left. The apartment building looked… tired. Like it had been walking forever and decided it had to stop right here in this city and take a break but then never managed to get up and move on. Oddly, this comforted her. Her own shoulders sagged. Her life in Pennsylvania had made her feel dilapidated, and this little building seemed to beckon her into its fatigue.

While the building did look like the pictures online, they must have been taken many years earlier, possibly after a significant renovation that had now weathered. The uneven walkway leading to the leasing office ended at a red wooden door with a lion's head door knocker. She moved up the walk, avoiding all the cracks and lines in the sidewalk, a habit she hadn't managed to grow out of.

Shiloh moved to pull open the door, but it didn't budge. She readjusted her stature and then used all her body weight to heave. The antique brass hinges creaked as the solid wood panel labored open.

The inside looked even more exhausted than the outside. The overstuffed sofa sagged listlessly in the middle of the room, and the dark, mahogany coffee table seemed wildly oversized given the modest size and condition of the other furniture. Floor-to-ceiling bookshelves lined the walls, which gave the place the feel of an old library rather than the lobby of a cheap apartment building. Her inexplicable sense of comfort deepened.

As Shiloh tried to reconcile the surrounding room with her expectations, she neglected to notice the tiny woman behind the monstrosity of a desk tucked in the back corner until a commanding voice startled her from her trance of admiration.

"Hello, Shiloh. I am glad you made it," boomed the brisk, female voice.

Shiloh jumped, swiveling her head side to side until her eyes settled on the petite figure. She stared, trying once again to get her bearings. The woman stood no taller than five feet, and her enormous, black-rimmed glasses were cartoon-esque. Shiloh might have laughed if it weren't for the woman's odd, maternal presence that seemed to command respect. As she approached, her bob bobbed, which made Shiloh smirk a little.

"I expect you found us alright the first time considering you are a whole one hour and thirty-six minutes earlier than expected?" Despite the question in her voice, the woman's coolly confident tone left no room for an answer.

"Hello," Shiloh responded suspiciously. "I didn't realize my arrival was so anticipated." She hoped her sarcasm masked her senseless nervousness.

Without a response, the woman surveyed her, narrowing her eyes a bit before spinning on her heel to beckon Shiloh back into an unobtrusive doorway. The small room could have served as an excellent closet, but instead Shiloh faced an expansive wall of keys. They were real antique brass or silver, not the key cards or small cookie-cutter keys cut at hardware stores. These looked like relics, works of art even. The woman searched the wall following an indecipherable pattern, and then it began to move like a conveyor belt. The belt whirred, faster and faster before stopping short with a clang.

"Exactly how many units do you have here?" asked Shiloh hesitantly. "That seems like an awful lot of keys." The wall showed no fewer than fifty keys at any given time and she found it impossible to estimate the size of the conveyor system.

"Ah, we have seventeen units," said the woman, who still had not offered her name. "A small number but with countless possibilities." She winked and yanked a key unceremoniously off the third row from the bottom. "Finally! Not sure why it took me so long to find it. I know this place like the back of my hand most days."

Most days? Shiloh found this an odd comment, but before she had time to inquire further, the woman handed her the key.

"My name is Margaret," she proclaimed.

Margaret carried on a bit about rent and due dates and such, but Shiloh let her mind drift, preoccupied. Everywhere she looked there seemed to be a detail she hadn't noticed before, each odder than the last.

None of the numerous light fixtures matched and the mix of finishes created an eclectic yet creepy vibe. Something about the shadows seemed to follow her even though nothing physically moved. A huge, Renaissance-style sconce barely lit one wall while a bright, modern glass globe adorned another, providing enough light to function, but not enough to truly see the crevices of the room.

"Alright, that's all for now," finished Margaret dismissively. "I trust you can find unit thirty-six on your own?"

"Wait, unit thirty-six?" Shiloh said, snapping back to attention. "I thought you only had seventeen units."

"We do," replied Margaret.

"Then why is my unit number thirty-six?"

"Why not?" asked Margaret, unconcerned as she took her seat behind the massive desk.

Shiloh walked back to her car and began slowly driving around the building. The units were labeled in a seemingly random fashion, first twelve then seventy-two then forty-one then two. She continued scanning for thirty-six, musing over the quirkiness of the building. Despite not even knowing where to find her apartment, she already felt excited and intrigued.

She steered the clattering trailer around the corner and finally saw number thirty-six on the far west corner. The festering anxiety lodged in her stomach dissipated, and she allowed herself a grin. All the parking spots in front of the first-floor walk-out unit sat open, allowing her car and its trailer enough room to comfortably slide in next to the building.

She sat for a moment, observing the chipped, potholed parking lot and path leading to unit thirty-six. The black door offered a stark contrast to the red brick façade of the building. A small patio with only half of a railing around the edges stared back at her, inviting her to come and adorn it with furnishings.

As she opened the car door, she heard a deafening crash and let out an involuntary scream. About five units away, the back of a blue sedan jutted violently from the brick exterior of her new apartment building.

Shiloh blinked incredulously, attempting to clear her vision of the strange scene before her. How could a car be stuck in a building? It looked like something out of an action movie. Then the gravity of the situation sank in.

Seeing only the car, she stumbled into a sprint. Before she could reach the accident site, though, another crackle of crunching metal halted her in her tracks. A second, identical vehicle, smashed into the back of the first car. The two cars bled together, mangled nearly beyond recognition.

This is absurd. I must be dreaming.

Shiloh scrunched her fists into balls and willed herself to wake up. For a split second she could have sworn the second car shimmered, like a mirage, but once she rubbed her eyes, the same horrific scene lay before her.

Not knowing what else to do, Shiloh continued toward the cars, slowing to a walk. She scanned the streets for signs of more cars or more wreckage but saw none.

Peering into the passenger side window of the first car, Shiloh glimpsed the driver, draped unnaturally over the steering wheel. One of his arms protruded out the window and his head had lodged halfway through the windshield. A desperate desolation washed through her as her stomach tied in knots. She couldn't fix this or even make it fractionally better.

The blank stare on the man's face left no room for doubt. He was dead, a look of terror frozen on his face.

Shiloh had never seen a dead body outside of the true crime re-enactments she streamed endlessly. Despite all her exposure from the shows, the real thing disturbed her senses in a way she had never experienced. The detachment provided by the screen and droning narration fell away leaving a raw, gruesome scene in front of her. This horrifying moment of death felt far too intimate for public viewing.

Adrenaline pumping, Shiloh stepped back and looked to the second car. Without needing to approach, she could tell the second man suffered the same fate as the first. Eerily, like the cars, the men looked so similar they could have been twins. She fumbled for her phone to call for help, but to her surprise a small crowd had gathered behind her. Unsure what to do, she glanced at one of the onlookers who seemed to be trying to organize the chaos and keep the crowd at bay.

The wail of the sirens rose to a deafening volume just as Margaret's tiny frame appeared from around the corner of the building. Scurrying toward the scene, she promptly took control of the situation, whisking the arriving firemen and police officers to the smashed vehicles.

Although Shiloh was sure Margaret had not been present for the crash, the leasing manager knew exactly how to handle the situation and began detailing, with remarkable accuracy, how the terrible wreck had unfolded. Pointing and gesturing, she spared no details. Without pause, she turned to Shiloh. "Did I miss anything?"

Still shell-shocked, Shiloh shook her head numbly and turned her back to the scene, unable to watch it for a second longer.

CHAPTER 2

The darkness curled its tendrils like an octopus of fog, slowly embracing and then engulfing the light around it. The sun, the moon, the stars, none could escape. Progress, though slow, continued, steady and unrelenting. Despite the cold wind sending chills through his gaunt frame, the babe quieted as the comforting dark soothed his cries and rocked him to sleep. He appeared to be alone in the world. Destiny vowed to keep him that way, the cool mountain autumn air his only company.

CHAPTER 3

As soon as she was excused by the authorities, Shiloh returned to her car and retrieved the antique key for her unit. She slowly opened the door and wondered how such a heavy, ornate key could belong to such a flimsy door.

The small, sad front room matched her mood after the horrendous accident. The high windows throughout made the place feel like a basement, despite being a first-floor apartment, and an overarching darkness hugged the space. Like the leasing office, none of the mismatched light fixtures that clung to the ceilings and walls seemed to emit quite enough light.

The paint on the walls, faded and defeated, peeled down by the baseboards. Although the hideous green carpet had likely been laid before she was born, it wasn't in horrible condition. A narrow corridor directly across the room led to a door, which she opened expecting to find a bedroom. Instead, the hallway ended in a dead end with a small closet. The other side of the room opened into the cramped, bare kitchen flanked by a tiny three-piece bathroom and a bedroom more appropriately sized for a walk-in closet.

Odd layout, but okay.

She sat down in the middle of the living room and heaved in a deep breath. Looking around this sad, tiny apartment waned her enthusiasm for her new start. Given the suddenness of the move and her inability to lay eyes on this place before committing, maybe she wasn't in a position to complain, though.

Sighing, Shiloh hoisted herself from the floor and started her long afternoon of unloading. She held the front door with her foot as she carried precarious stacks of belongings, but a twinge in her back sent a jolt down her spine every once in a while. She made a mental note that a dolly would be a worthy investment for the next move. At least she was getting her exercise in for the day.

By 5 p.m. boxes had consumed her dimly lit apartment. In her haste to get out of her old place, she hadn't bothered labeling and had no idea where her clothes and dishes might be entombed in the pyramid before her. Joe had been calling at persistent intervals all day, and she had finally thrown her phone across the room to let the mess swallow it.

Even from across the country he knows how to be an asshole.

Pizza seemed like an absolute necessity before making any big decisions, so she placed a quick order and then started with the boxes closest to the kitchen. She turned on her audiobook, an obscure mystery novel recommended by one of her favorite Instagram accounts, Literary Litmus, and resettled into a rhythm.

She unboxed surprisingly quickly. Chipped dishes and a trusty blender highlighted her kitchen collection. In the living room, her stained rug from college felt undersized, even in this notedly small apartment, but it would do. The eco-activist in her swelled with pride just a little bit at her thrift. She didn't need to buy more. She had everything she needed.

Lost in the comforting monotony of organizing, she continued until the sight of her mother's old Tiffany lamp snapped her rhythm. Its crooked shade and broken pull stared up from the half-empty packing box. The dank apartment air seemed to swirl around her despite the stuffiness she felt. Even though the nostalgia always stung the same, it surprised her how swiftly it bubbled up when she looked at the tattered reading light.

She hesitated for a moment and then walked the lamp down the dead-end hallway and stuck it on the top shelf of the coat closet. She didn't have any end tables for it to rest on, which assuaged her guilt just a little. The lamp was ugly anyway.

Shiloh went to one of the few boxes she did label and dug out a well-loved physics textbook from her favorite course in college. She had always felt dorky, but she truly loved that book. It had opened her eyes to the world of physics and helped her uncover not only something she was good at, but also something that sparked joy during a hard time. She had been stressed and broke and feeling unsure about absolutely everything, but when she buried herself in that course, she escaped to a world that made perfect sense. Although challenging, physics always had an answer. Right or wrong, black or white. She craved that certainty in her own life, so anytime she could find just a little bit of it, she thrived.

A piece of junk mail turned bookmark tucked under the cover fluttered to the floor. Shiloh rolled her eyes. This fake university that she could only assume played a part in an elaborate scam would not let up on the direct mail campaign.

For years she had received fliers and letters no matter her location, but when she searched Revned University online no results populated.

Exhausted, she finally came across the box containing her bedding and took this as a sign it was time to for bed. Shuffling down the hallway, she flipped the switch for the hall light. The space transformed into a scene from a haunted house. The bulb strobed, highlighting a stained, drooping shower curtain and loose towel rack through the open bathroom door. She jumped and fumbled to flip the switch back off, unsure why the flashing light unnerved her as it did. She didn't necessarily mind the dark but had to admit this nook of the apartment felt eerily dim. She'd need to replace that bulb.

After a quick, lukewarm rinse in the dilapidated shower, Shiloh collapsed into a heap on her bed. She had nearly drifted to sleep when her eyes snapped open. Her planner. Where was it? Had she accidentally thrown it out with the trash?

She sprang up and out to the kitchen, using her phone's flashlight to see. She rummaged through haphazard piles of stuff, growing increasingly more agitated. Then she spotted a tattered purple corner, sticking out from under a stack of mismatched dishes on the counter. The fluttering in her stomach slowed as relief flooded through her core. Grabbing the notebook-sized planner, she added "lightbulb" to her running grocery list and then went back to bed and fell asleep in record time.

The next morning, gray light streamed into her eyes through the small bedroom window. Momentarily disoriented, she held a hand up to shield her face until the events of the previous day flooded back, shocking her into alertness.

The walls seemed exceedingly tall from this vantage point, and she couldn't help feeling a little claustrophobic.

Pulling on some joggers and a sweatshirt, Shiloh splashed water on her face before heading out the door to make her first grocery store run.

No time to waste.

She got all the way to the car before realizing she forgot to check the type of lightbulb the hallway fixture needed. Irritated with herself, she turned the ignition off and scurried back into the apartment. The chair she stood on wobbled precariously as she struggled to unscrew the flush mount's dirty globe. The frosted glass stuck to the ceiling, and she had to jiggle the base before it finally came loose in her hands.

Inside, a collection of dust bunnies, dead flies, dirt, and a folded-up piece of paper collected into a gross little pile. Repulsed by the dead, rotting bug corpses, she dumped the contents into the trashcan. Then the itch of curiosity struck, and she reluctantly fished out the piece of paper. Just to make sure it wasn't anything important, she told herself. The yellowed slip held a short, sloppily scrawled note. "I cheated on my twelfth-grade math final so I would graduate valedictorian. Nobody suspected a thing."

Chuckling to herself, Shiloh let the note fall back in the trash bin. Confessions of a guilty conscience, an interesting methodology for absolution, but alright. The knowledge that a previous resident felt the need to leave a secret behind made the apartment feel a little more personable.

The rest of the day passed quickly as she ran errands and continued settling into her new place. She went to a local Goodwill and found a wire bedframe, a set of curtains, and a small table and chairs that she managed to shove in the back of the trailer she hadn't returned yet.

As she worked, the boxes slowly dissipated, and the apartment started to feel a bit more spacious and less confined. The sixty-watt lightbulb she bought neatly slipped into place in the hall light fixture.

That night, she again fell into a quick, deep sleep without even trying. She dreamed of being transported back to high school. Finals week had arrived. She'd been studying for hours on end but still didn't feel prepared. Between her three AP classes and her advanced calculus math course, the pressure continued to squeeze tighter and tighter. A girl, who Shiloh didn't know in real life but was her best friend in this dream world, sauntered up.

"Oh my gosh, y'all, I think I totally crushed my English final. I'm so relieved. That essay topic—soooo easy," drawled the girl in a sweet Southern accent. "How was your biology final? Do you think you did well enough to steal the valedictorian spot from Ken?"

Shiloh slammed the locker shut while struggling to zip her backpack. "Oh, yeah. Biology went great. I'm most nervous about calc. This semester I've been so caught up in other classes I've just been skating by. I have that one next. If it goes well, I think I can grab valedictorian. Wish me luck."

"Good luck, you got this!" cheered the girl enthusiastically.

Shiloh walked down a hallway that seemed to never end before turning into a classroom with only five students in it. The bell rang, and she slipped her pencils and erasers out of her backpack. The teacher handed out the exams, wished them luck, and praised the class for a wonderful year. The students all knew each other well and before settling into the task at hand they exchanged nervous, excited grins.

Fifteen minutes in, Shiloh was making good progress, but the material grew harder with each question. She concentrated and then without even thinking about it peeked at a cheat sheet slipped up the sleeve of her shirt. She didn't remember putting it there, but it seemed like the most natural thing in the world. Everyone else in the classroom, including the teacher, was too wrapped up in their own tasks to pay her any attention in the back corner. As she moved through the test, whenever she couldn't recall a formula or next step, the information in question waited literally right up her sleeve.

At the sound of the bell, Shiloh sighed, relieved to be scribbling the last line of her final equation. She stood up and shyly brought the test to the teacher.

"Thank you. It's been such a pleasure teaching you this year. I know you'll do great things. I'll be rooting for you for valedictorian."

Grinning ear to ear, she left the classroom and headed straight for the doors of the high school. She aced it and didn't feel one little bit guilty about the help from her notes.

As the dream faded, she entered the strange place between sleep and waking and willed herself not to get up yet. The peaceful sleep had been so nice, and the pride swelling in her dream still felt so real. She dozed just a bit longer before opening her eyes to a bright, but much thinner stream of light peeking through her new bedroom curtains. Lying in bed, she thought back to the dream. She hadn't thought about high school in years, let alone testing.

The premise of the dream perplexed her. She had been an excellent student but no valedictorian and hadn't really strived to be. Her priorities had lain elsewhere, and she had been entirely content working toward for perfect grades though not quite always succeeding. She had certainly never cheated her way to high marks. The one time she had was in elementary school on a silly assignment and the guilt still haunted her to this day. She surely would never have cheated on something as important as a final exam without feeling any remorse at all.

She rolled over, pushed the odd dream from her mind, and drifted back to sleep.

CHAPTER 4

As the darkness thickened, it set its sights on a new horizon. In space, to build strength, the dark must engorge as much of the universe as it can. It is no different on Earth. Darkness is defined as the absence of light. It is the power to paralyze or to cause chaos. It is control.

The perfect balance of light to swallow and dark to shield happens every evening. Unobstructed progress can be made by lurking in the shadows. So the toddler became a shadow, followed by darkness wherever he went.

CHAPTER 5

<hr>

Shiloh flipped on the hallway light switch and the crisp brightness emitted from the brand-new bulb gave her a tiny thrill of satisfaction. Then she remembered her strange dream. Until this moment, she had forgotten all about the confession note in the light fixture but was now sure it had burrowed into her subconscious somewhere and caused her mind to fabricate the scene.

This realization fascinated her. For someone who felt like she was constantly forgetting things, she wondered at how her mind could retain the most insignificant details and resurface them in such interesting ways. She had always found the mind and the study of psychology a mysterious and poetic balance of art and science. Paired with her love of writing, Shiloh had always secretly, very secretly, fantasized about becoming a poet and exposing the mysteries trapped inside the human condition. But it hadn't been practical.

Deep in her gut she knew that mind-set could be partially credited for the abrupt shedding of her previous life. Practicality had suffocated and confined her, and she couldn't trust those closest to her to care. They would never take her seriously, so how could she?

Maybe her exit had been somewhat dramatic. If nothing else, the twenty-three missed calls from Joe showed just how many loose ends had been sharply cut rather than neatly tied. Somehow that didn't seem nearly as important as she thought it should, though. It drained her, trying to reconcile what she should feel with what she actually felt.

The sound of coffee dripping to the floor interrupted her train of thought, and she cursed as the hot liquid splashed onto her toe. Unplugging the pot, she reached for a paper towel and mopped up the mess. As she stood, a zap sounded above her head and flashes of strobing light inundated the kitchen. The dank space with its coffee drenched counter and overflowing trash danced, taunting her.

She gasped, flipping the light switch off. "Why am I not surprised?" she muttered. She would have to make another trip to get yet another lightbulb today.

Hopping into jeans and a T-shirt, an upgrade from her wardrobe choice yesterday, she walked out the door to make her second run to the store in as many days. Although she knew many people who loathed spending time at the grocery store, she didn't really mind it. With a good audiobook playing and a list in hand, she ticked things off like a pro, fostering a disproportionate sense of satisfaction given the simplicity of her charge.

She perused the aisles slowly in an effort to orient herself to the unfamiliar layout while navigating through the list in her purple planner. As she walked, she found herself thinking about the irony of the small things. In her previous life, grocery shopping had been a relatively quick project, completed nearly on autopilot with the floorplan of the store embedded somewhere she couldn't quite put her finger on.

Her gaze lingered on the coffee. The sweet, fresh scent of ground beans emanated down the aisle, and she paused to inhale deeply. A small smile edged the corners of her mouth. The lovely, wafting aroma of fresh beans brought her back to early mornings in her childhood, watching her parents consume multiple home-brewed cups a day. She allowed the wave of nostalgic longing to take over, just for a minute.

Out of habit, she looked for the familiar local roasts from Pennsylvania, catching herself only a second later. She was a creature of habit, but Joe had loved trying new coffee. When they first moved in together, Shiloh had spent entirely too long in the coffee aisle considering which new type he might like best and how she imagined it would taste with the flavored creamer he loved.

Oh, how the times have changed.

* * *

Her new city still felt exotically foreign, and she made sure to take in the surroundings and identify landmarks to navigate by. She drove by the side of the building where the crash happened only a couple of days ago and shuddered, remembering the coldness of the dead man's eyes. A combination of industrial grade Saran Wrap and caution tape sealed the gaping chasm in the exterior of the building. The residents had been assured that the integrity of the structure remained intact, and that they were all safe in their units. She briefly wondered who lived in the apartment that had so dramatically lost its wall.

By the time she pulled back into her parking space in front of the apartment, the sun had started to set. Foolishly hanging all her grocery bags onto her arms at once, Shiloh hobbled up to her door aiming to avoid a second trip out to the car. Upon getting to the door, she realized she couldn't manage both the key and the bags and had to let the groceries plop onto the concrete. Shoving the door open and grabbing her bags even more hastily than before, she stumbled into the dark front room, groping for the light switch. The buzz of a giant housefly rang in her ears as she rummaged through her bags to find the economy pack of lightbulbs.

Pulling her chair under the flush mount in the kitchen, she again jimmied the globe until it gave way and allowed her to unscrew it from its resting place. This fixture looked no cleaner than the last, and to her bemusement she saw another note settled at the bottom of the bowl.

Carefully avoiding the dead beetles and the brown specks of bug dung, she lifted the piece of paper and unfolded it. This note, in a similar scrawling hand to the one before, read, "I killed my class pet."

She dropped the note, as if creating a physical gap would somehow make it go away. Another confession. She had to admit, this one mildly disturbed and intrigued her. After all, who in the world would think to leave notes inside light fixtures?

Weird.

Shrugging off the uneasiness, she pried out the old bulb, which was screwed unnaturally tight. She replaced it with the new brighter, LED version and resecured the bowl. With that task complete, Shiloh stared at the mountains of half unpacked boxes and tried to decide where to restart.

She stood, paralyzed by options, and thought about how often she felt like this—like the possibilities available to her were so numerous she couldn't possibly pick just one. What if she chose the wrong one? What if she wasted her time? Or worse, did something that would later come back to bite her? She realized the ridiculousness of applying this mind-set to her unpacking situation, but she couldn't help it. When she looked at her life wholistically, all the worst-case scenarios seemed imminent.

Then she caught herself. This outlook, this type of thinking represented yet another reason she left her old life. She wanted desperately to be free of this paralysis, and she knew a big life change would be necessary to make it happen, or at least start her in the right direction.

When she decided to make this move, Shiloh had promised herself she would do more of the things that made her happy. So instead of continuing to unpack, she chose to go for a jog and then let her audiobook lull her to sleep.

* * *

In her dream, she was transported back to the school again. Somehow, she knew it was the last day of classes, but this time she was younger, maybe in middle school. The feet of this strange dream body took her to the science classroom to pick up Gertrude.

"Come on, Gerdie," she cheerfully smiled at the hairless rodent in the cage. "We're going to have a great summer."

As she skipped out of the building, nearly floating on her end-of-year high, a familiar knot clenched deep in her stomach. She operated on autopilot, moving toward an unfamiliar house she knew to be home in this world.

Scurrying up the sidewalk in front of the house, she failed to see the step right in front of her. The toe of her shoe caught on the concrete, and she sprawled to the ground, Gertrude's cage flinging into the wall. The animal squealed in pain, and

Shiloh scrambled desperately to find her. To stop the sound. Terror filled her chest when she saw tiny Gertrude's two back legs splayed at unnatural angles. The tortured screeching continued, and tears blurred Shiloh's eyes as she tried to cover her ears. She couldn't take it.

Nobody was home to help. She scrambled up the stairs inside the house, Gertrude's mangled cage in hand

The massive snake glimmered under the red light of the heat lamp. Horror filled her gut. She knew she was about to do something terrible yet was powerless to stop it. The snake looked up and flicked its tongue at them with a small hiss.

In one bite, the wailing stopped, Gertrude gone.

CHAPTER 6

———

The darkness feeds on uncertainty. Did you know that? It knows when light is already in danger and capitalizes on the opportunity. It recognizes a single misdeed, a single dark thought, and coaxes a little bit more, and a little bit more after that…

Darkness stalks like an all-powerful predator. It stays constant when nothing else, nobody else, does.

He filled his lungs with the comforting blackness of the Colorado winter evening. Breathed in his favorite time of year.

In the night, his fragile skin could not be burned, and the bullies could not find him. He could slip away from home, that horrible place with those appalling parents, without a trace. He was not missed. Nobody could miss someone as useless as him.

So his little heart sang as he watched the sun set.

CHAPTER 7

With a good night of sleep under her belt and only a fraction of her boxes left to unpack, Shiloh felt more upbeat than she had since the horrible crash. She decided, on a whim, to turn up her favorite music and dance. She had seen women in movies do it after particularly difficult moments in life, so why not? She belted out the lyrics to her favorite Madonna remix and let the unboxing absorb her attention.

Bang, bang, bang.

Loud rapping on the apartment door caused her to jump. Breathlessly pausing her music, Shiloh sank back into the bedroom, unsure of who might be there. The tone of the knock didn't sound friendly. Maybe they would just go away if she didn't answer.

She crouched, listening.

Then Margaret's shrill voice sounded as clearly as if she were standing in the apartment. "I know you are in there, Ms. Shiloh. Open this door right now. I am your landlord, and hiding in the corner like a terrified antelope will not make me go away."

Sighing heavily, Shiloh pulled a T-shirt over her sports bra and opened the door. Margaret stood on the stoop with her arms crossed. Two men loomed behind her.

"Well," bristled Margaret. "I hope you are not here to pursue a singing career. That was dreadful. Please do remember the walls are thin and you have neighbors."

"Yeah, erm… Hi. What can I do for you Margaret?" Shiloh focused sheepishly on her feet and fiddled with the bottom of her T-shirt, trying hide her reddening cheeks.

Without waiting for an invitation, Margaret stepped into the apartment and surveyed the contents. The men followed, wordlessly. "Well, at least you are attempting to unpack."

Shiloh shifted, unsure why Margaret's five-foot stature projected such an intimidating presence. The landlord began nosing about the living room, poking her head around corners and into half-unpacked boxes, not even trying for subtilty.

Without pausing her inspection, Margaret announced, "Shiloh, Larry and Richard have joined me today. They are here from the engineering division of the state permitting office to inspect the entire building after the unfortunate accident earlier this week. An impact of that magnitude can have far-reaching consequences, you know."

Surprising even herself, Shiloh snapped back, "Of course. I have a master's degree in physics and am quite aware of the implications of high-velocity impact on an older structure."

Margaret turned to survey Shiloh, one eyebrow raised. She continued, "Since the building will need extensive repairs on one side, we thought it only wise to check out the other as well."

The two men resembled ducklings as they mirrored Margaret's every step. Despite their muscled bodies, they seemed unable to venture out on their own.

"Please," said Shiloh hastily. "Feel free to inspect whatever you need. I apologize for the mess. I'm still getting settled."

Margaret nodded and waved the men down the hallway to start their survey.

Once Larry and Richard entered the bathroom and seemed to be out of earshot, Margaret approached Shiloh and asked, "What do you remember, exactly, about that day? You were the only eyewitness." Her gaze had transformed from composed and nonchalant to scrupulous and suspicious in a matter of seconds.

"I just remember hearing the first car crash and running to the wreckage. Before I could get there the second car collided with the first." Pausing, Shiloh replayed the events in her head. "The entire building seemed to quiver, and I could feel it, even without being inside. And the cars… I thought I imagined it at first. They were so… similar. The cars could have been the same make, model, color, and year, and the men could have been twins."

Margaret stared at Shiloh like she had lost her mind.

Unsure, Shiloh added in a smaller voice. "There were two cars. Right?"

Margaret didn't break her gaze but hesitated before replying, "Only one car. You must have been in shock. Your mind can play tricks on you in traumatic situations, you know. The man's name was Gary Schneider, and his blood alcohol level was 0.31 percent when he crashed. Frankly the authorities are not sure how he was conscious, let alone operating a vehicle."

Shiloh remained silent, grasping for her knowledge of blood alcohol levels. Frankly, it wasn't much. She turned to Margaret, skepticism growing. "Wait a minute. You led the police to the scene and told them exactly what happened without sparing any details. How did you do that if I was the only eyewitness?"

"Silly girl," Margaret said, brushing her off. "I simply told them what I *surmised* had happened based on my observation of the scene. I did not even pretend to have witnessed it myself. Really, dear, you seem very confused. Maybe this affected you a bit more than you thought. You should just take a few days to unwind. The stress of moving and then witnessing such a tragedy must be a shock to your system."

Shiloh waivered momentarily. "But…" she stuttered. "I saw you recount everything exactly as it happened."

"Well maybe things are, in fact, exactly as they seem," Margaret smarted back. "The power of observation is unmatched, if applied with experience." With that, she called to her men and twirled on her heel. She marched out the crooked door frame, not bothering to wait for them.

Larry and Richard scuttled out behind her, nodding at Shiloh as they left.

"Thank you," Margaret shouted from down the sidewalk with a small wave of her hand.

Perplexed, exasperated, and irritated all at once, Shiloh stood rooted to the floor. The anxious part of her brain that never quite turned off prodded for more information. She craved answers, and Margaret's matter-of-fact explanation of the crash did not satisfy this itch.

On the other hand, the landlord might view Shiloh asking more questions as an unwelcome intrusion, and she didn't want to start any drama. She didn't want to ruin her chance at the carefree life she desired by getting sucked into the vortex of those around her quite yet. She knew she could trust herself, but no one else, to protect her newfound freedom.

CHAPTER 8

He always took the hard road. Trudging along the path to the schoolyard, he counted not the trees lining the way but rather the shadows he could distinguish. Much more difficult than counting trees. Trees were simple, solitary creatures, he thought.

Twelve, thirteen, fourteen… *thud*. His head hit the dirt and a powerful shadow fell over his body. The faceless bully laughed and kicked and whispered horrible names in his ear before moving along. Lying motionlessly, the boy cried silently before looking up to find he was alone again.

He turned around and walked away from the school building, weaving deeper and deeper into the woods until the sun barely shone through the thick foliage. Here he stopped and opened his library book about forestry.

Soon, immersed in the world of the woods, he lost track of time. He paused to reread several times when he came upon a chapter about Pando, the great aspen grove of Utah. The concept of a mycorrhizal network fascinated him beyond anything he had imagined in his ten years of life.

Apparently, tiny root tips joined trees together underground and allowed them to not only share nutrients, but also

to communicate with each other. The cover of the soil shel-
tered them from the harsh light and weather. That safe haven
allowed the roots to confide in each other, like a close-knit,
compassionate family joined both physically and spiritually.
The concept was entirely foreign and entirely fascinating.

Trees, it turned out, did not exist independently, he
mused. Under the cover of darkness, they were secretly one.

He longed, more than anything, to be a tree root.

CHAPTER 9

The apartment looked like a tornado had ripped through with reckless abandon, but Shiloh exhaled a tired, satisfied sigh of relief. *Finally unpacked.* Empty boxes lay scattered in a mosaic across the shaggy carpet. Items piled high on the vinyl counters nearly touched the low ceiling, but that didn't matter. She held her head high and surveyed the scene. Her tenacity had paid off.

The old Shiloh let her belongings languish in boxes for months on end after a move and spared no opportunity to make herself feel guilty about it. Every time she went to retrieve something she would promise herself to get unpacked the next weekend. Nevertheless, the cycle droned on unbroken. The small stuff had overwhelmed the old Shiloh, but not anymore. She was starting over.

She considered the accumulation of circumstances that had snowballed into the tipping point of her former life. Insignificant, unrelated events that mildly irritated her had smushed together over time to form a rapidly growing mass barreling toward her. She had found herself constantly awake in the middle of the night, perseverating on mundane things like her grocery list as Joe, blissfully unaware of her turmoil, snored beside her. Her brain attempted to reason, but she couldn't stop obsessing, despite their fully stocked pantry and fridge.

This puzzled and frustrated her to no end. She woke up groggy and foggy, attempting to tackle her day with only a few hours of restful sleep. Once, the stress had become so overwhelming she melted into a full-on panic attack over her to-do list of three items. The panic-inducing list consisted of folding clean laundry, dusting, and mailing a letter.

Knowing she needed a change but unable to pull herself out of the riptide that sucked her down, she left. Before leaving, she had, unsuccessfully, floated the idea of relocation with Joe, testing the waters.

"Why don't we go somewhere new? Try something different? We're young and free. Let's just try," she urged.

He hadn't even bothered to look away from his video game. Instead, he laughed at her. "You're a pain in the ass just trying to get our shit together to go on vacation. Why would I want to try and pick up our entire lives?"

Wounded by his callousness, Shiloh retreated to the bedroom. When he finally joined her, he told her she was being stupid and overly sensitive before rolling over and promptly falling asleep.

The memory still stung.

This exchange had been the last straw. Reduced to tears in the shower, she finally acknowledged just how miserable she felt. Three days later, she signed the paperwork for her one-way U-Haul rental.

As if on cue, her phone lit up. Joe. As much as she didn't want to answer, it was probably time.

She hit accept, bringing the phone to her ear without a word. He didn't even wait for her to say hello. Instead, he burst into a string of angry expletives and accusations. Not once did he ask if she was alright or why she left.

So typical.

"Joe, you're a toxic, emotionally abusive prick. I want more, and I deserve more. I'm not in love with you, and I did what I wanted to do for once. I don't care what you think anymore. Don't call me again." With that she hung up and deleted his number from her contacts.

Surprisingly energized, Shiloh made her way to the bedroom and flipped the switch as she entered. Eerily familiar strobing startled her, and she jumped about three feet in the air. Rolling her eyes at her own skittishness, she tried the switch a few more times with the same result.

"This is ridiculous," she muttered under her breath.

Standing on the wobbly kitchen chair once again, Shiloh jiggled the outdated light fixture until it broke free. The stuck and blackened burned bulb forced her to wrestle with it before finally popping loose, and a piece of paper fluttered to the floor. She could hardly believe it. One note was strange, two a coincidence, but three? Three was a pattern.

She hesitated, torn between her curiosity and her desire to brush the notes off as nothing.

The dirty slip of paper beckoned, though, its yellowed corners curling up like grasping fingers. She unfolded it.

"I buried my mother's murdered corpse."

An electric shudder ran down her spine. Who the hell had lived here before? This had to be someone's idea of a sick joke. Even so, she dreaded sleep.

That night she fought to stay awake, but the darkness crept up and transported her to a black and starry night. Her feet shuffled along a muddy dirt path until she came to a large weeping willow. The tree drew her in, as if pulling on an invisible magnet lodged in the pit of her stomach. The normally comforting smell of rain failed to sooth the dread manifesting inside her.

As the moist brush flattened beneath her boots, she quickened her pace but not by choice. A puppeteer seemed to move her limbs in this stilted forward motion. Her body slammed into a wall of leaved branches, parting the way into the private space between the trunk and the outside world. Her blood ran cold as she registered the horrendous scene before her. She wanted to scream, run, and cry all at once, but the puppeteer propelled her right up to the lifeless, bloodied female corpse.

She fought the movement but no matter how hard her mind resisted, her actions remained mechanical.

Screaming on the inside but muted to the world, Shiloh took the slender ankles of the body and pulled, leaving a path of muddied blood beneath the willow. She paused to look inside a large, hollow notch in the tree before working her way to the other side of the canopy and moving into the tall underbrush. Her stiff neck swiveled to obsessively check the path for any signs of other humans. The night remained deserted, though, the soft hooting of a lone barn owl the only sign of life.

A pre-dug grave lay before her, about six feet deep. Shiloh lined the pale body up next to the hole before rolling it in. Bile rose to her throat at the soft thud of the body. The woman's red hair fell in last, reminding Shiloh of a flame, snuffed out by the dirt. She piled earth back into the grave with relative ease, her biceps surprisingly strong. Her body shoveled relentlessly even as her mind fought to understand her actions.

Once she had completely covered the corpse, she moved back along the bloody brush, kicking at it clumsily to hide the crimson river pointing like a neon arrow to the grave. As she distanced herself from the tree, the leaves began to shake and rumble. Swaying like a sailor without sea legs, the tree's branches rose to the sky, sucked into a vertical wind tunnel.

The willow waved and bowed, and the large notch Shiloh had noticed before the treacherous burial morphed into a mouth-like structure, gasping for air. Involuntarily, she stopped and watched, awestruck. The power of nature and the power of something else altogether collided.

Finally and suddenly, as if giving up, the wind retracted, and the tree collapsed into a tired droop once again. Shiloh followed suit, falling to her hands and knees in the thick brush. Her core stayed stiff as if it were the trunk of the tree.

Shiloh snapped her eyes open, sweat soaking her shirt at the nape of her neck. Blinking rapidly, she sat up and jumped off her mattress. The early morning light left her room dimly lit.

It took a second to get her bearings, and she momentarily forgot where she was. Slowly, relief began to quell her fear, wrapping around her like a blanket as her new life came flooding back. Her heart raced but worked to slow itself.

Ripping her soaked shirt off, Shiloh shakily made her way to the bathroom to hopefully wash away the horrible nightmare. Its vividness left her shaky. She couldn't remember ever feeling so immersed in a dream.

She undressed, let her hair loose, and turned the shower handle all the way up, waiting for the poorly pressurized water to warm. When she looked down at her outstretched hand, she noticed the dark brown filth of dirt under her nails.

CHAPTER 10

As the clouds drew in above him, it felt as if the curtains were being drawn on the world. Despite his newfound maturity, the sixteen-year-old still found solace in the forest, just as he had as a boy.

The mood shifted and the tree-sheltered grove became intimate and sensual instead of energetic. It aroused him.

His confidence festered along with his desire, and he let his mind drift.

She had tugged him into the bathroom, pressing herself into the curves of his body. His heart pounded in anticipation of what was surely to come. Then, abruptly, she turned on the light and instead of undressing for him, she laughed. She kneed him in the crotch and left him wriggling on the floor like a helpless lamb instead of a fierce man. She took pleasure in his pain. Upon regaining his composure, he realized her snaking arm had stolen his wallet.

The sting of her rejection smarted like a fresh wound.

His anger had seethed, boiling over with the help of embarrassment and guilt. His limbs, including his member, pulsated. He did not think he could contain the rage that enveloped him.

He had screamed. Cursed. Thrown his fists into the walls. Then the lights went out, and the entire building had plunged into darkness.

Once again, it saved him. It knew how to infiltrate the most horrible situations and provide refuge. Provide cover. Under its blanket, he skulked out of the club's back door, casting a shadow of shame in all directions.

The memory ruined his mood and the privacy of the trees felt frivolous. He rolled over on the forest floor, disgusted by his own vulnerability.

CHAPTER 11

Even though the meticulously hand-scrawled sign on the door said the office didn't open until 10 a.m., Shiloh arrived at nine forty-five. Enough was enough. Emboldened by the dim light shining through the dirt-encrusted window, she shoved her way in, deciding not to wait until the posted opening time.

The dank but comforting smell of the bookshelves and leather couches embraced her dramatic entrance. Before she could launch into her indignant rant about proper electrical wiring, a pen levitated from the coffee table and whizzed past her head like a dart, skimming her ear.

"What in the world…" Shiloh had time to whisper-shout before a book followed the pen in hot pursuit. She dropped flat to her stomach, assuming what felt like some semblance of a combat pose. At that moment, a door at the back of the room slammed and a low pitch, barking laugh rumbled from the corner of the office. Shiloh lifted her head to see Margaret grinning smugly.

"What the hell are you doing?" Margaret asked in a patronizing tone.

"What the hell are *you* doing?" Shiloh shot back, unintentionally defensive.

"I," said Margaret, her voice dripping in matter-of-fact irony. "Am exercising my mind and practicing my controlled psychokinesis. And you?"

"Your what?" was all Shiloh could muster in response.

"Psychokinesis. You should be doing the same."

"You've already lost me." The words Margaret was stringing together meant nothing to her. "I don't know what you're talking about. You sound loony."

"There are far worse things than being loony, my girl." Margaret chuckled. "Stop playing with me. Surely you have heard of the science of psychokinetics?"

"No, as a matter of fact I have not," Shiloh snapped. She didn't like feeling stupid. "I came over to make you aware of an electrical issue in my unit and, apparently, defend myself against flying objects."

"Such a drama queen," Margaret chided under her breath. "You have so much to learn. Do you really have no idea?"

"No idea about what? I know my lightbulbs are strobing out daily and turning my apartment into a circus fun house. This leads me to believe you need to check your wiring and get someone out here to fix it, so I don't go broke buying lightbulbs." Shiloh's mind spun with frustration. Was she dreaming? Margaret's intent, genuinely curious gaze left her unsettled.

At this, Margaret laughed almost heartily. "Oh Shiloh, the electrical is not the problem. The problem is you."

"I know how to change a lightbulb," retorted Shiloh without hesitation.

"Of course you do, my dear. Oh my. I thought you were playing coy… clearly an erroneous assumption on my part. We have much catching up to do. How much time do you have?"

"Well, I don't have a job or a life at the moment, so pretty much all of it."

"Great," replied Margaret, reverting to her business tone. "Step back into my office here and I will explain it all." She flipped the leasing office sign to "closed" despite the early hour and trotted back into the shadows, not bothering to make sure Shiloh followed.

Feeling marooned but curious, Shiloh made her way back to the corner nook that held Margaret's huge mahogany desk.

Instead of sitting at the desk, the older woman perched on the nearby ancient leather couch, looking like a spring ready to uncoil. "I am so glad you are here. We have much to talk about. Wine?" she asked gesturing at a brass bar cart.

"Umm… sure?" Shiloh replied, raising an eyebrow. She hadn't pegged Margaret as the drinking type, and it caught her off guard. "You do realize it is 10 a.m.?"

"So?"

"I still don't understand…" Shiloh tried to start.

Margaret half-smiled again and cut her off, setting two glasses of red wine on the coffee table. "And that, my girl, is why I am here."

Shiloh squinted, waiting for elaboration.

"Do you ever think about things you don't seem to have any control over, good or bad? I mean really ruminate on them and then, all of a sudden, one day they happen?"

Shiloh froze. "Yes… I'm sure it happens to everyone. Manifestations of your feelings or willpower, or maybe both I don't know."

"Did you never wonder *how*, though? How your thoughts could actually formulate into events? I bet your fancy physics degree cannot explain that. Can it?" Margaret asked earnestly, waggling her finger.

Shiloh barely breathed. "Yes. I mean I've wondered occasionally… Mostly, though, I believe in Karma, and I just sort of figured…"

The older woman rewarded Shiloh with a look that likely passed as a beaming smile for Margaret. "Yes! You believe! Good! That means you have at least a primal understanding of the forces beyond your control. For the time being."

Shiloh eyed Margaret warily. "I'm still lost."

"Come on. You are smart enough to understand. You just choose not to. Do I have to spell it out for you? Even with all those big textbooks, surely you cannot believe you know everything there is to know about the world?"

"Well, of course not, but my field of study is black and white, so excuse me for not decoding your riddles. I just want my lightbulbs to work!"

"I have never heard a more ridiculous statement in my life. Nothing about physics is black and white. And *certainly* nothing about neurophysics is defined that clearly, so we may have more learning to do than I thought."

Shiloh was ready to lose it. "For your information, neurophysics is not even a real and reputable field of study. You don't have any idea what you're talking about. Are you planning to fix the lights, or do I need to call someone myself and send you the bill?"

Scoffing, Margaret looked at Shiloh quizzically. "Real? Reputable? Those words have no meaning. Just because you cannot understand something does not mean it does not happen. I made that pen fly with my mind! That pen is definitely real. Was it just lucky that it did not nail you in the forehead? I think not. I never miss! You witnessed your first psychokinetic connection today. And before you protest, I would like you to read this book." She heaved a giant volume up to her waist and then let it thud heavily onto the oversized coffee table.

"Please read it. Truly take the time to absorb it. Smell it if you must. After you finish, come back, and I have every confidence that we will be able to fix your lightbulb issue."

As Margaret continued her quick, nonsensical prattling, Shiloh sensed a presence next to her ear. Turning, she smacked her eye right into the corner of the thick book hovering beside her.

Falling back in disbelief, Shiloh glared at Margaret who cupped a hand over her mouth to stifle a laugh. The book remained untethered and unbothered, surrounded only by empty air.

She stood and plucked the book out of the air with both hands and then spun to leave. The bell on the heavy door tinkled behind her chased by Margaret's quiet giggle.

CHAPTER 12

If she could just do something, anything right. As he stood, shielded behind the dark velvet curtains, the shadows kept his position concealed despite the harsh light emanating from every room. It felt like living in a fucking Christmas tree sometimes.

The scene played out as if he were watching on television.

The pounding footsteps.

The slurred cursing.

The unlatching of the closet door.

The click of the gun locker.

The bang of the shotgun.

The silence.

He didn't need to bear witness to the scene to know what had happened.

His father threw the gun, another bullet ricocheting upon impact with the floor. "Clean this up, boy. I don't want to see it in the morning."

The door slammed, and a sputtering engine roared to life.

The clacking of tires disappeared over the hill, and the seventeen-year-old came out, consciously averting his gaze from the mess in the next room. He turned off all the lights and closed his eyes, protecting his unadjusted vision for as long as possible. But he couldn't block out the smoky, metallic odor of blood and gunpowder. He was strong, though. His strapping form had begun to take shape, and his mother weighed barely one hundred pounds.

He hoisted her over his shoulder and walked all the way to the old weeping willow. She sat against the massive tree and rested, waiting for him to do his part.

He dug, making sure her final resting place would be dark enough to stamp out the memory of her horrid life. Her horrid death.

Dumb bitch.

The nest he made for her would protect her from evil, or at least that's what he liked to imagine. He dragged her into the hole and gazed at her one last time. The fiery red of her hair disappeared last. As he shoveled the final bit of dirt back into the grave, light peeked over the horizon. The dark had stayed when he needed it most. It shielded and cradled him, so he did not have to bury his mother alone.

The night couldn't... wouldn't betray him.

He didn't understand why people turned on the light when they were scared. As if the expulsion of dark would prevent whatever horror awaited them. The light exposed you; it gave away your position. The light could not protect you, only quicken your demise.

CHAPTER 13

———

The old problem, a ghost in her new life, resurfaced. So many, paralyzingly many, choices. Shiloh had begun looking for employment online, but all the openings sounded as mundane as the one she had left behind. Not to mention, she had no idea what she actually wanted to do. The more potential jobs she found, the higher her frustration and stress levels climbed.

She had a very real and somewhat urgent need to find a source of income, though, so she submitted her résumé for a part-time dog-walking position. She loved dogs. That could be low stress. Right?

With that out of the way, procrastination was no longer an option, and Shiloh couldn't thwart her curiosity. Despite her better judgment, she resigned to throw herself into Margaret's reading assignment whole-heartedly. She flipped through the faded cover as well as several blank pages before finding the title, *A Synopsis of the Mind: Physics, Neuroscience, Cognitive Science, and the Interconnectedness of the Psyche.*

The author was listed by one name only: Roya. Below the name a picture of a dream jumped off the page. Shiloh understood the strange symbol instinctually, even though it felt impossible. Strictly speaking, the drawing depicted an outline of a square with a squiggled line through the middle that looked like the output of an EKG machine. Vertical equal signs straddled either side of the line inside the box, forming an odd but definitively dream-shaped picture.

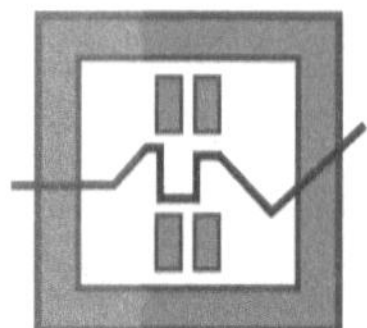

It irked her. She stared, trying to understand how her eyes could see only the simple combination of lines on a page, yet her mind could translate it into logic so easily. She could have sworn the depiction had never been in any of her textbooks, but she recognized it all the same. When she stared, she saw so much more than just a dream, but she had no language to describe it. Sensory inputs flooded her brain, evoking raw emotion in her the same way a memory might.

Fascinated and puzzled for the hundredth time since her arrival to Denver, she flipped the page and began to read. After only a few moments, the book had her hooked.

The text started with the history of cognition including both folklore and scientific origin explanations. The biologic details enthralled her, and for a moment, Shiloh wished she had majored in biology. Then she got to the physics section and was in her element. She hadn't really focused on the biological application of physics, but it fascinated her.

The book manufactured images and equations demonstrating how extremely low levels of electricity flowed through everything, including the human body. As she read, she did the math, and it checked out. Her mind floated and jumped like she was trying to learn her way through a fantastic land. Except she knew that wasn't the case. Roya's logical connections astounded her; however, just like the symbol at the beginning, Shiloh followed every jump and understood why it all made sense.

The next assertion took Shiloh completely off guard but also, paradoxically, did not surprise her at all. Electricity did not have to be contained into any single vessel or organism, she read. These tiny, sometimes nearly undetectable currents of energy that flowed through living organisms could not be created or destroyed. Even upon transfer. In other words, everything, in theory, could connect to everything else.

A lightbulb turned on in her head. Of course. Somehow, she had known this at a primal level, but to see it written and proven so elegantly before her… she couldn't believe her eyes.

How did I not realized this sooner?

The density and complexity of the text continued to thicken, but Shiloh blazed through, too keyed in to think about the passing of time. She had always learned quickly in school, but this was different. Like a sixth sense, her mind began making leaps on its own. The blocks of scientific text simply stacked into place, fitting together as naturally as Legos.

The next section narrowed its focus significantly to only the human brain. The brain, it turned out, when harnessed and trained, was the single most powerful computer on Earth. It even controlled the body by sending electric signals throughout.

Most humans poured all their energy into executive functioning and trivial, everyday tasks, but the brain was capable of so much more. If the mind were to harness and channel the available energy from the surrounding environment, its power was theoretically limitless. It could control things beyond the body using something called psychokinesis.

Her mind turned over like the uneasy waters of a stormy sea. As skeptical as Shiloh felt about the strange, imposing woman, she needed Margaret. The topics in this book made her own intuitive suspicions about Karma and the universe feel real, and she sought validation. She couldn't reconcile this new knowledge with her existing understanding, nor could she push it away. You couldn't ignore science.

Although some of these later conclusions were theoretically impossible by the standards of physics she had studied, Shiloh knew the book was not a whimsical fantasy or a fictitious novel to get lost in. Margaret had harnessed and controlled electric currents to psychokinetically manipulate the pen and the book before Shiloh's very eyes. This was real. And the implications were immense.

Shiloh had more questions than answers, and she didn't sleep for even a moment that night. The tossing and turning spurred her to reread passages by flashlight. She realized she could have turned the light on, but she was supposed to be sleeping so that just felt wrong. This was a childish notion, but she didn't care. Notes in tiny handwriting began filling her planner, but she made sure to only use the page for the current day. She had to stay anchored.

When her cheap digital alarm clock finally read 6 a.m., she couldn't pretend to try and sleep any longer. Shiloh sprang out of bed, the first goal of the day to clear her mind. Despite physical exhaustion, running always did the trick, so off she went.

She loped along struggling to find her rhythm, the runner's high just out of reach. She mildly regretted the long route before her breathing slowed and fell into sync with her pace. Not too fast, not too slow. Nice and even. Eventually, her brain caught on, and coherent questions for Margaret started to form.

After her loop, she jogged past the office just in case Margaret happened to be in early. To her surprise, the faint green illumination of the desk lamp glowed through the grimy window. Nearly tripping over herself, Shiloh stopped short and stared at the door, willing it to open. She thought of the door opening. She prayed for the door to open. She even thought about running at the door to try and move through it like they did in the fantasy books she loved to read. Before she could try this last idea, though, the door creaked open, and a hand poked out, beckoning her inside. Margaret stood in the middle of the dim room appraising Shiloh over the tops of her glasses.

"You were not seriously going to try psychokinesis four hours after finishing *Synopsis*. Were you?" she quizzed, one eyebrow raised.

Shiloh avoided her gaze. Instead of launching into her list of well-formulated questions, her mouth opened into an avalanche of unintelligible words. "But, erm, how, I, what, it doesn't… I don't…"

Margaret let out a full belly laugh, surprisingly low and hardy for such a petite lady. She began to recite a long but clearly practiced speech in a low tone, as if calming a frightened kitten.

"The thing you need to know, is that it is all true. Every word. I have either witnessed or experienced all of it first-hand. Not everyone is lucky or disciplined enough to harness the power of their mind, but I believe you can. As you might imagine those who discover their currents and how to wield them possess incredible amounts of power that can be used for incomparable good or insufferable evil. As you also might imagine, people have chosen both paths although not with equal success."

Shiloh wrestled with this thought for the first time. She felt stupid, but the ramifications of this knowledge and power in the wrong hands had not crossed her mind. She quivered at the thought. Dumbly, she simply stared at Margaret. What was she thinking letting herself get caught up in such a hoax? If all this truly existed, why hadn't she learned about it, at least at a cursory level, in school?

As if reading her mind, Margaret scolded. "You're the physics whiz. You should know this. You know better than anyone that energy cannot be created or destroyed, only transferred. Your brain transfers more energy, more quickly than any other organ on this planet. Where do you think it goes?"

"It's used by your body. Obviously. That's kind of the whole point..." Shiloh smarted back.

"Some of it," Margaret responded evenly.

"What the hell does that even mean? I'm not falling for it. I know I'm gullible, but this is a whole new level of crazy." She turned, ready to walk out, but the heavy door slammed before her, forbidding her exit. Margaret hadn't moved.

"This is most certainly not a joke. Believe it or not, there are things in life that even you and your precious professors do not understand yet."

Shiloh flopped on the couch, closing her eyes in frustration. All this had been so much more believable at 3 a.m. "If we're going by the book, people can actually decide how to release their own energy? So instead of products of our environment, we're like intelligent live wires with universal plugs?

We can use the electricity within us however we choose if we can learn to control it?"

"Finally!" snorted Margaret. "The lass catches on. Took you long enough."

Shiloh continued her train of thought. "So if everyone on Earth has this power, why doesn't anyone know about it?"

"I never said everyone on Earth can do this. That would be quite overwhelming. Besides, can you imagine what would happen if everyone knew? If everyone had expert control of the power of the human mind and body? The constructs that would fall? The chaos that would ensue?" Dryly chuckling Margaret continued, "For one, the planet would be a wreck and our governments would lose any semblance of power they currently hold. For the people with authority, it would be catastrophic. Since it is so hush-hush, a small fraction of us keep the art of psychokinesis alive. In return for our cooperation, the powers that be largely leave us alone. They consult us on major global matters of course, but for the most part we do not like to get political. We are scientists, same as you."

"And you think I can do it?" asked Shiloh, captivated.

Tittering, Margaret breezed across the room and drew the shades. She silently selected a book from one of the wall shelves and set it on the table in front of Shiloh. She looked at the title, hoping for a sequel to *Synopsis*. Instead, her face fell when she saw a tattered copy of *A Wrinkle in Time*, her favorite book, motionless on the table.

"Not everything can be learned from a book. To master this particular art, you must learn through experience. This is your favorite novel. What is your favorite page?"

Shiloh stared, "How did you know..."

"Never mind that," Margaret retorted, snapping her fingers in front of Shiloh's face.

"My favorite page? What kind of a question is that? I have no idea!" Shiloh responded.

"Ahh, yes okay. Let's just aim for the start of chapter eleven, page one hundred and ninety-four in this volume."

Without Margaret so much as flicking a wrist, the pages to the volume whirred into action, flipping so fast they blurred together into a cloud. Just as abruptly as the movement started, it stopped, and page one hundred and ninety-four stared up at them.

Shiloh smirked and grabbed the book, closing it again. This didn't look that hard. She relaxed, cleared her mind, closed her eyes, and focused on page one hundred and ninety-four, picturing it in her head. She stood motionless for moment, unaware of everything else around her until Margaret burst into laughter once again.

Irritated and embarrassed, Shiloh looked at her. "I have no idea what I'm doing!"

"Just because you want something to happen doesn't mean you can just *will* it into existence. You must use your electric current to spur that of the book. I have not taught you how to do this yet, but I want to see if you can figure it out. Give it one more try."

Shiloh closed her eyes again and examined her body in a way she had never done before. She let all her anxiety and trepidations about this strange situation float away. Soon, her heartbeat intensified and then, an ever-so-slight tingle in her fingers came to life. They felt like they were about to fall asleep, but she knew they were not.

As she focused, Margaret began to coach her. "Yes, don't forget to breathe. Lean into the sensation."

"I feel it! It's a tingle in my fingertips," Shiloh exclaimed, snapping her connection.

"Why did you shift your focus? Get it back!" Margaret urged, throwing her arms in the air.

Shiloh rolled her eyes and started over.

"You must start, as you did by emptying your head of silly thoughts and unimportant matters. Every distraction must go. Then find your own body's electric current. All our currents are slightly different, like fingerprints." Margaret paused to appraise Shiloh's demeanor, her gaze cutting like a blade.

Shiloh dared not break focus again.

"The easiest place to feel your current is in your extremities. Sometimes you may feel it accidentally, for example when you shock yourself, but most of the time you probably do not even notice it. Mine feels like a tiny buzz, but research shows the sensation differs from person to person."

A smile crept across Shiloh's face as the almost-asleep feeling returned to her fingers. A page of the book lifted a fraction of a centimeter. It might have been a breeze from the ceiling fan.

"Brilliant!" Margaret praised. "Next, you must feel the energy of things outside your own body. Objects are easiest to start, but eventually I will teach you to find the current of living things too. You also have a natural affinity to the energy of the things you love, like this book in your case. You will need to stay physically proximate to the target object while you learn. As you get stronger, you will be able to perform psychokinesis from further away."

Shiloh touched the book lightly and a tiny jolt shot through her fingers.

Was that it?

"Remember, channel first your own energy and then let your mind venture to the book. Consider its physical properties like mass and weight and then shift to the atomic structure of the book. Find the energy between the atoms."

At first, nothing happened. Shiloh allowed her fingers to explore the precious book, feeling the texture of the cover and the lightly crinkled corners. Then her tingle began to buzz and reverberate just a fraction. Inexplicably the book pulled her closer without physically moving her body at all.

Margaret, seeming to intuit the connection, murmured barely perceptible words of encouragement.

Confidence growing, Shiloh took a deep breath and allowed herself to plunge deeper into her own energy. What felt like a thousand volts of electricity shot from the book, and it sprang to life. Unlike Margaret's demonstration, the pages churned erratically, chugging and flapping rather that whirring. All the same, they flipped. Shiloh sensed the book changing with each page turn. As her excitement grew, though, her connection both with her own energy and that of the book unraveled.

"Ouch!" Shiloh exclaimed. The break stung like the snap of a rubber band.

Margaret clapped in three short bursts in front of her face. "That was exquisite! Given your lack of experience, you exhibited an unprecedented level of control over your subject. I knew you would catch on quickly. We need to keep up your practice. There is no going back now."

Margaret resumed pacing about the room and Shiloh suspected her incapable of staying still.

"I want you to come here in the evenings. I will teach you. At home you need to practice holding on to your tingle, as you call it, for longer and longer durations. That is step one. You will exhaust yourself if you try to do it all at once, but eventually awareness of your own energy will become second nature. You should also practice connecting to and manipulating inanimate objects, like this book. That skillset will be absolutely foundational and only just the start of what you can accomplish, young lady."

Shiloh swelled in spite of herself. Her old self lived for compliments from those in positions of authority. She considered whether Margaret was in such a position and found herself looking up to the older woman as a mentor. Even though they barely knew each other, Shiloh's trust grew rapidly. She knew she could be good at this.

CHAPTER 14

Rain poured from the heavens. The clouds moved overhead in anticipation of his arrival and shielded him from the targeted rays of the setting sun. Others ran for cover, but his arms opened wide, embracing the onslaught. The tiny pin pricks of rain brought out the best in him. He relished the chafing of wet jeans between his thighs; every step like sandpaper, scraping off his outer shell.

The Revned University theoretical cognitive science building loomed, its spires resembling the teeth of an angry black bear.

Massive doors swallowed his angular frame upon entering. He kept to the side hallways and avoided the open grand staircase out of habit. His office lived in a dark and lonely corner with no windows. Brass hinges creaked, and his dark eyes flitted over his co-inhabitant's desk. Disgust and hatred simmered in the pit of his stomach.

The paper. The wrappers. The overflowing trashcan. The tidings of a disgraceful slob.

Motion flicked in the corner of his vision. The man turned over on their shared office couch, sleep unperturbed by the squalor to which he was subjecting the entire area.

Waste of a human.

If you cannot take care of your own space, you should not get your own space.

Flipping off the light, he packed the meager belongings from his desk neatly into the safety of his bag.

Under the guise of darkness, he lit a match, hastily threw it in the trashcan and left the building as quietly as he had come in. Just before the double doors slammed in his wake, he heard a faint explosion.

He laughed in delight.

CHAPTER 15

The ringing of her phone interrupted Shiloh's peaceful morning social media scroll. Nobody had bothered to call since she told Joe off. Groaning, she looked at the lit-up screen. "Unknown Caller." She absently picked up.

"Hello, hello!" chirped a female voice on the other end not bothering to wait for a response. "My name is Amy. I'm happy to offer you a job with the Rover Dog Walking Consortium! Honestly, we're swamped, so if you're still interested, could you start today?"

Shiloh sat up, pleased about this tiny bit of good news. "Yes... I'd... yes, of course," she stammered, still wholly unprepared for a full-length conversation so early in the morning. "Thank you!"

"Great! Wonderful," Amy replied. The woman didn't come up for air. "Download the app. I'll text you instructions. Sign up for as many walks as you can handle. Remember, we expect at least three dogs per day to get walks. We always say the more the merrier, so if you can take multiple dogs together, all the better. I won't keep you on the phone any longer but will email you paperwork to sign. Get back to us ASAP, please and thank you!"

Before Shiloh could formulate a response or think of any questions, the line clicked. Perky Amy hung up. Perky people made her tired.

From her bed, Shiloh looked over at her ugly desk lamp. She would never have kept it, but she hated being wasteful. It worked perfectly well after all.

Events of the past twenty-four hours flooded her mind in an overwhelming current of unbelievable information. She dropped her head in her hands and closed her eyes. It all felt so real. Was it real? Panic rose in her chest.

Breathe.

Maybe she could just test it out. She found the tiny, barely perceptible tingle in her fingertips. Cautiously, she tried to find the lamp's energy and feel the current pulsing through it.

Bang!

She jumped, squealing in horror. Two black, beady eyes bore down through her window, so sharp they could almost cut right through her skin. Through the glass, a dazed crow stared back at her. Then it flung itself at the window. Over and over, the creature flew manically, desperately, into the glass.

She leapt back, scooting against the wall on the other side of the room. It must have rabies or something. This logical explanation did not ease the dread manifesting in her core.

Seemingly in response to her thoughts, the crow gave one final thrust and then flew away on a drunken path to settle onto an elm tree across the street.

"What the hell?" she muttered. She'd never liked birds.

As her heartrate returned to normal, she refocused her attention on the lamp. Strangely, the tingling warmed her from the inside out. It hadn't been a dream.

Focus aimed at the gold pull cord of the ugly lamp, she directed her willpower and her tingle toward illuminating the room. The lamp wobbled precariously, and Shiloh's heart leapt into her throat.

No, no, no, no, no.

The lamp collided violently with the floor, and she peered cautiously at the mess. The only thing broken besides her ego was the bulb. Both relieved and disheartened, she picked up the lamp, careful to avoid the shards of broken glass. Yet another one to replace.

Shiloh moved about the apartment mechanically, muddling around and adding to her to-do list for the day. She needed to go see Margaret, but she also had to get a start on her new job so perky Amy didn't fire her. Time to get a move on.

She walked briskly, picking up her day's canine charges one by one. The physical exercise, as usual, relaxed her whirring mind. She hadn't actually gotten a straight answer from Margaret on how the burned-out bulbs had anything to do with psychokinesis. Margaret seemed to know it all, but how helpful had she really been?

If she took everything the strange woman said at face value, the world was a much different place than Shiloh knew it to be. Her thoughts drifted to *Synopsis*. Despite seeing the described phenomenon in real life and even trying her own hand at psychokinesis, it all still seemed unbelievable. It was becoming apparent that the existing world differed dramatically from the one she understood.

The wind picked up and Shiloh snapped back to reality. She'd been walking for over an hour and now found herself spectacularly lost.

Some things never change.

By the time she dropped all the dogs off at their respective homes with their especially grateful owners, the clock read four thirty. She headed to the leasing office where Margaret waited at the door. Instead of a traditional greeting, Margaret welcomed her with a steady stream of questions about her psychokinesis practice.

Shiloh dutifully reported out her progress including her mastery of the page-turning exercise and the movement of small objects. Her frustration with the lamp still stuck fresh in her mind and overshadowed her triumphs, though.

"You know," Shiloh followed up. "This is amazing, unbelievable stuff, but I don't understand how studying psychokinesis is going to fix my lights. Can I manipulate the current in the lightbulbs and keep them from burning out?"

"Do not be foolish. You cannot stop a lightbulb from burning out." Margaret laughed.

"Why can't you just fix them like a normal property manager? Is that too much to ask?"

Margaret seemed to enjoy making her feel stupid, and Shiloh hated it. She wasn't accustomed to being the one in the dark and didn't like it one bit.

"My suspicion is that you have been unwittingly shocking the bulbs with your high voltage, unharnessed energy and causing them to burn out," explained Margaret with a smirk. "Now that you are working on controlling this, your bulb situation should improve."

Shiloh reflected on this theory for a moment. "Do you know who lived in the apartment before me?"

"Yes…" Margaret replied, eyeing Shiloh curiously. "A little old lady named Mrs. Winslow. She unfortunately lost her mind and had to be sent to a nursing home for people with dementia. It was quite sudden. Lucid as a cat on the prowl one day and then batty as a wombat the next."

"Batty as a wombat?" Shiloh couldn't keep the giggle out of her voice.

"Yes! It is true, if you have never met a wombat, you would not know. They are quite ludicrous creatures."

"Hmm… was she ludicrous enough to leave notes in the light fixtures?" Shiloh asked, satisfied by the puzzled expression on Margaret's face.

"Notes? What notes?"

"They're weird… almost like diary entries or confessions on little slips of paper. So far, I've found one in every light fixture with a bulb issue." Shiloh hesitated. "The last one was pretty dark… it talked about killing someone. And then I had the most vivid, horrible nightmare. I buried a body." Shiloh shuddered at the memory.

Margaret stood still as a statue. "Nightmare, you say?"

"Yeah. I've always had vivid dreams, but these are… I don't know… different. I feel like I'm someone else."

"How many have you had?"

"Three so far. One after each note I've found…"

"I must see the notes this instant," said Margaret, grabbing Shiloh's hand and propelling her out the door with surprising force.

Shiloh turned to Margaret in alarm. "What's wrong?"

They scurried down the sidewalk, and Shiloh kicked herself for brushing off the gut-sinking feeling that followed the discovery of each note. *Stupid.* Her trust in herself had never been as great as her trust in others.

Shiloh reached for her key, but by the time her hand emerged from her bag, the door had swung wide open.

"Keys are simply a formality to offer people who do not understand psychokinesis a false sense of security," Margaret informed.

Shiloh made a mental note to inquire more about that statement later. She started rummaging through used dust wipes, pizza crusts, and shards of broken lightbulbs in her kitchen trash to find the notes. Finally, her fingers grasped a grimy piece of paper, and she held the first one above her head in victory.

An anxious Margaret hopped to snatch the slips as quickly as Shiloh could dig them out, flattening them side by side on the vinyl countertop. She distractedly pulled a chair behind her to sit and then stayed silent for what felt like hours as she read the short notes over and over. Finally, she put her head in her hands.

Shiloh opened her mouth to again ask what was wrong, but before she could utter a sound Margaret's voice rang in her head telling her to stay quiet. Although the command was not given out loud, Shiloh shut her mouth.

The lights dimmed a fraction lower as the older woman peered around the apartment and swore, this time speaking audibly albeit under her breath.

Without warning, she thrust her flimsy chair back with so much force that it fell over as she met Shiloh's eye. "These notes are means to achieve direct brain-to-brain communication, the most powerful and most difficult psychomanipulation skill to master. It is the only explanation, though it feels impossible even as I say it. If I am correct, which I usually am, these nightmares are dark connections with a terrible person…"

"What are you talking about, Margaret?" Shiloh asked. The woman wasn't making sense again.

"Come with me. I think I have a bit more explaining to do," Margaret replied as she pulled the two of them out the door.

Shiloh had only ever been inside the leasing office, but this time Margaret walked straight through the cozy familiarity and up a narrow staircase hidden in the back corner.

How did I not notice that before?

The stairs groaned under the weight of Margaret's small frame, and Shiloh hesitated. As if intuiting her feelings, Margaret beckoned impatiently for her to proceed.

Upon emerging on the second floor, palpable relief washed through Shiloh. She found herself standing in an even more comforting version of the downstairs office. Bookshelves covered every available vertical surface and papers confettied every horizonal one. The large desk in the corner looked as if it could swallow Margaret whole, just like the one downstairs, but here Shiloh could tell the older woman was in her element. Margaret moved nimbly through clutter and switched on a kettle.

"Tea. We must have tea. We have a rather long night ahead of us, my dear. I need a hot drink in hand to think clearly." She scooped up a host of papers and books to make space on the couch and patted it, signaling for Shiloh to sit.

Sinking into the cracked leather, Shiloh couldn't help but notice the most ornately understated chandelier she had ever seen dangling above her head. It had no fewer than a dozen bulbs, yet the delicate bronze candelabra produced a comforting warm glow, not at all overpowering despite the small size of the room.

"A gift from my best friend. She had an affinity for light fixtures. I have had it for many years, and even so, it still brings me immense joy," explained Margaret, catching Shiloh's gaze. "I do not have much of an eye for design myself, but she always did."

Margaret paused to look up at the chandelier. "She is gone now."

"I'm sorry," Shiloh replied softly. "How do you do that?"

"Do what?"

"Anticipate my questions. Respond like you're reading my mind. I had the strangest experience when we were in my apartment. I was about to speak but heard you tell me to stay quiet, even though you didn't actually say anything."

"Ah, that. A form of brain-to-brain communication. I am not able to read your mind, but I can read your energy. Along with that skill, knowledge about your personality and body language allow me to deduce your next move," said Margaret, enjoying the chance to step back into her teacher role. "Echidnas do it, you know!"

"What's an echidna?"

"Oh, you know, a spiny anteater. They use tiny electroreceptors on their snouts to find and hunt prey based on sensed electromagnetic currents and known behavior."

"Seriously? You essentially know what I'm thinking, and you're just now telling me?"

Ignoring her, Margaret continued, "Since you are starting to get the hang of finding an object's energy, the next step will be sensing and harnessing the energy of other living beings. It is not easy, but it is also not as complicated as it may seem."

"So, like an echidna?"

"Exactly. Brilliant. In fact, once you know how to focus, it bolsters both parties' currents to become much more intense. It is all up here," she said, tapping Shiloh's forehead with her index finger. "You see, your mind is both your most powerful and most versatile tool."

The kettle whistled, and she paused, motioning for Shiloh to go tend to it. Embarrassed for not helping the weary-looking Margaret sooner, Shiloh scurried into the kitchen and brought back two aromatic mugs of steaming black tea.

"Fortunately, or not, that is what brings us here tonight." She paused, as if for dramatic effect. "I must tell you a story.

I want to be clear; it is not a story I am proud of nor one that I enjoy telling but the time has come."

Shiloh waited motionlessly.

"It started when I was much younger than I am today. I had nearly completed my PhD in psychokinesis at Revned University and volunteered to mentor a younger student. Many doctoral candidates are expected to do this, you know. His name was Draven. Despite his young age, he showed an aptitude for the subject. Brain-to-brain communication, a theoretical concept at the time, held particular interest for him. His research took him deeper and deeper into the rabbit hole and soon, I admit, he had surpassed me. I tried my damnedest to meet him where he was at and answer all his questions or at least guide him in his quest for answers." She paused. "But I failed." Avoiding eye contact, she focused on the wall behind Shiloh.

"It is just that... he absorbed new information way faster than the typical student. He drank from the proverbial fire hose, and he took it in stride, caring not that he was soaked and chilled to the bone day in and day out." She shook her head and stroked her eyebrow nervously.

"He soon became understandably frustrated that mentors like me could not teach him what he wanted to know. Finally, one day, his short temper snapped and, not knowing what else to do, I brought him to meet my best friend."

Then she looked at Shiloh, as if pleading for her understanding.

"The one who gave you the light?" Shiloh ventured gently, trying to nudge her along.

"Yes." Margaret smiled tightly. "That is the one. She had also just finished her PhD, but instead of practical psychokinetics like my degree, she specialized in theoretical psychomanipulation with a concentration in direct brain-to-brain communication. She had high hopes for grand purposes like bringing world peace and reversing climate change. Not to age myself, but this was the seventies, so the hippie movement was thriving. I admired her dream and envied her academic prowess. I was smart in my own right, but she was downright brilliant."

She paused, looking at Shiloh expectantly.

Shiloh had no idea what to say, so she just replied. "I'm sure you are just as smart."

Margaret gave her a strange look and then waved it off. She continued her story although hesitantly.

"Anyway, her and Draven became closer and closer and spent more and more time working together. Over those next few years, I began to resent the pair of them. It is just that I felt… left out… and a bit elementary for not keeping up if I am being totally honest. Together those two completed the very first successful brain-to-brain communication, a historic moment for Revned University and the field of psychomanipulation."

Shiloh continued to sit still, enthralled in the story. That university name sounded so familiar, but she couldn't quite place it. She would have to ask Margaret where it was located.

"Then things shifted. My beloved friend met the man who would become her husband. She began to make plans for a new life, but one problem threw a wrench in things. Over the course of their working relationship, Draven had fallen madly in love with her. When she left, altogether rejecting his advances, things went downhill fast for him."

"Devastated by her departure, the odd and short-tempered Draven became reclusive and secretive. It turned out he had taken on a private project of his own. His new obsession became finding a way to use brain-to-brain communication to render control over the world around him. A magnificent risk and ethical travesty. Revned dismissed him promptly upon finding out, and I never heard from him again."

The narrative had completely captivated Shiloh. Questions whizzed through her mind as her imagination filled in the gaping holes in Margaret's story. It played like something out of a novel.

"Where did he go?" Shiloh asked.

"I did not know, nor did I really care at the time, if I am being truthful," Margaret replied. "I had been in a bit of a slump and was very wrapped up in myself, unfortunately. Serendipitously, or so I thought, my friend had written and said she needed help with a project, so I packed a bag and headed to Pennsylvania for a visit. And that brings me to my point."

"Pennsylvania? That's where I'm from…" A chill traveled down Shiloh's spine, but Margaret cut her off, as if afraid of losing steam in her story.

"When I arrived, I could not believe the state of her. She looked completely wired. Her anxiety held her captive in her own home, and she had recently started having awful nightmares. She hypothesized that Draven was somehow communicating with her via direct brain-to-brain connection. Despite her best efforts, she could not keep him out completely, and she needed my help. She knew her deteriorating mental health was starting to affect her husband and young daughter."

"I did not believe her at first and tried to reason with her, but I eventually gave up and did the only thing I knew would help my friend. We researched and devoured all the scholarly publications at our disposal, including those sent to us from my Revned colleagues. She convinced me to look for a way to sever his direct connection. Ultimately, though, we were unsuccessful."

"After a three-week stay, I had to accept my part in the failure and return to the university, tail between my legs."

Sorrow and regret filled her eyes as she sighed.

"A few weeks later, I got a call that she was missing. Her suitcase was gone but only few of her belongings were absent. A manic letter arrived in my mailbox a few days later and confirmed my suspicions."

The dread in Shiloh's stomach blossomed into panic.

"She had decided enough was enough. She had decided to face Draven head on. I felt so… ashamed. If only I had not abandoned her." Margaret bowed her head, shaking it back and forth. "She would not have given in to him in her right mind. I tried everything I could think of to track them down but to no avail. I had no leads, and her letter gave no indication of their destination. Eventually I lost hope."

"My desk…" She nodded toward the corner of her apartment. "Is dedicated exclusively to finding the two of them. Twenty years have passed, and I have grown desperate. Nothing new has been found for so long. Until your notes and their manifestation. It has to be him."

"But why me? Why my apartment and not yours?" Shiloh asked cautiously. The story rolled around in her mind like a marble, but it still wasn't fitting together.

"The same reason I wanted you here." Margaret paused as if steeling her nerves. She inhaled sharply, rose to her feet, and began hastily straightening the overflowing bookshelves.

"That's sweet, Margaret, but we've only just met," Shiloh teased, trying to lighten the mood. "I like you too, but I ended up here randomly. I picked this city from a hat and this apartment from a google ad."

Margaret put her face in her hands. "I am making a blithering idiot of myself. Not like me at all. I have one more piece of critical information."

She spread her fingers to make a small opening with her hands, peering at Shiloh with one eye. "That is not strictly true. I mean the random part… I may have… erm… influenced… your decision, to move here. To Denver. And also, your apartment choice." She winced as if Shiloh might strike her.

"That's impossible," Shiloh retorted haughtily.

"Have you learned nothing? I can manipulate almost whatever I wish and for the things I cannot, like Google, I have techie friends, Wendel and Simon, who can. I do not believe in chance and neither should you. I wanted you here. And here you are. You are smart and capable. It is in your genes, after all."

Before this move, Shiloh had thought of herself as unflappable, but here she sat, stunned yet again. She wasn't sure whether to be furious, indignant, astonished, or glad. Somehow all these feelings bubbled up at once.

"What do my genes have to do with anything? You don't know anything about me. You can apparently influence anything in the world to your liking, so why me?" she blurted.

Margaret's eyes shone glassy. "Because your mother was my best friend, Mariam."

Shiloh gaped. Fragments of information swam through her mind, starting to formulate an impossible picture. Then the lights flickered, and the space was pitched into complete and sudden darkness.

For a split second the apartment stayed eerily silent, but as if on cue, the lights flickered back on as Shiloh began to respond.

"After my mother left, my father refused to say her name, let alone talk about her. I had always thought, or hoped, or maybe felt that… I don't know… that she wasn't dead. We never had a funeral, even though she was presumed dead. My father refused to do it without… her."

Margaret scooted across the oversized sofa and gently cupped Shiloh's hand in hers. The look she gave Shiloh contained a nearly unbearable level of sympathy.

Hot shame burned in Shiloh's stomach. She should have known. Somehow, she should have known.

"I loved and respected your mother like a sister. I also looked up to her, emulated her, and envied her all at once. Sadly, after days, then weeks, then months, and finally years without word, I have come to accept her demise."

Silence permeated the small space while Shiloh raked her fingers over the worn texture of the couch and stared deep into the fibers of the rug. She made them tremble with her mind. The tingling sensation in her fingers soothed her. "So… she's really gone?"

"I am afraid so, my girl. I am so sorry."

Shiloh grabbed for the arm of the sofa as the room began to spin.

CHAPTER 16

Electricity, nearly visible in its intensity, flowed freely from his body into the charged atmosphere. Without moving his head from his hands, he used his mind to slam the book shut and fling it at the wall. The volume took such a blow that a few pages separated from the binding and fluttered helplessly to the floor. His psychokinesis embodied the frustration coursing through him. As his anger pulsed, so did the lights.

How could he be expected to achieve greatness if this idiot, Margaret, refused to answer the most fundamental of questions? Was she truly stupid or just a recalcitrant? Clearly, she couldn't see his potential.

The answers existed beyond theory, whether she would admit it or not. Brain-to-brain kinetic control had been successfully conducted and replicated at this university. They had the technology.

He was not supposed to be privy to this information, but their apathy toward his skill had left them vulnerable. He dampened his abilities in the presence of others and used their underestimation to his advantage. Like the darkness, undervaluation could protect you from the scrutiny that came with the spotlight.

Margaret began to speak, but he recognized the bud of an excuse before it left her mouth. He didn't care what she had to say. He was beyond her.

Roaring, he threw her desk lamp against the wall, smashing the bulb. He nearly impaled her with a pen.

Her face whitened as fear shut down the armor she used against him.

He could not work with this imbecile.

He needed Mariam. Only she could be his equal.

CHAPTER 17

Clouds outlined in shimmering gold floated across a cotton-candy pink and blue sky. Somehow both flat and dynamic, they beckoned her, soft and comforting as pillows. Shiloh watched, momentarily transfixed. Thoughts shimmered as her mind rested in a fugue. Her eyes settled on one cloud out of the corner of her vision, but the imposing corner of a dark and dusty bookshelf snapped her back to reality.

The air left her lungs, and the room wobbled, musty atmosphere squeezing instead of cradling her as the smell of old books usually did. She wheezed a few times and closed her eyes, taking a long, shaky breath. This time when she looked up, she peered straight at Margaret's eyeballs, magnified into saucers by her thick-rimmed glasses.

"Breathe, girl. Please do something useful with your lungs this time before you have another syncopal episode. I realize my delivery was not the best, and I apologize. Empathy has never been my strength, no matter how much I study the concept." Margaret sounded borderline panicked.

The walls groaned with the brewing storm outside and reverberated in sync with the anger pulsating in Shiloh's head.

"How could you not tell me? How could you trick me into coming out here, lead me into this rabbit hole, and then leave out the most crucial pieces of the whole equation? My life could have made some semblance of sense!" Shiloh accused, her voice trembling.

The bookshelves in the room seemed to collectively hold their breath. Her new jigsaw puzzle of a life was still missing a dozen pieces. Shiloh sat up and rested her head in her hands, trying to think. Trying to decide where to start.

The blindsiding revelation about her mother sliced open a wound she thought had closed a long time ago. She had sought answers for so long, but to have them splayed in front of her in such a raw and abrupt manner... She couldn't begin to articulate all of her conflicting emotions aloud to Margaret.

On top of the staggering personal blow, the need to pivot her world view and interpretation of reality yet again sent her into a tailspin. The decision to come here had felt like hers and hers alone, but it turned out her first move as the assertive and independent person she longed to be was actually just a set-up, founded on a secret family history that made no sense.

Intuiting Shiloh's emotional overload, Margaret jumped in. "I will answer any questions you have. We can take as long as you need tonight. But after tonight, we have to move forward. You need to move forward. Because I need you. If Draven is alive, just maybe Mariam is as well... If there is any chance at all that she is still alive, she needs you."

At this Shiloh looked up. Nobody had truly needed her for anything in a long time.

Then Margaret's words hit her.

Mom might be alive.

She didn't trust herself to speak, so she just sat up straighter, her eyes darting and searching for something that would tell her how to respond.

Margaret looked flustered and started waving her hands dramatically as she spoke. "Given your recent experiences, I have reason to believe his abilities have grown to extraordinary levels and that he is capable of unspeakable acts of terror. I thought we had time, but this contact suggests otherwise."

Margaret got up and began to pace in tiny circles. "It could mean one of two things. The first, and possibly lesser of two evils, is that he is close. Although he is dangerous, if he is close, we can find him. The second, more dreadful scenario, is that he has achieved an unprecedented level of brain-to-brain communication."

For the first time, Shiloh noticed the faded circle on the rug that matched Margaret's exact path. Finally trusting her voice, Shiloh squeaked. "Tell me about her. About my mother."

Margaret paused her pacing, pity registering on her face as her demeanor opened just a fraction. "Your mother was the most powerful mind our community had ever known. As I mentioned, we met at Revned University."

A flood of realization hit Shiloh. "I know how I know that place! I got letters from them for years, mailed to my home address no matter where I lived. When I tried to find information online, nothing came up, so I just started throwing the letters out with the junk mail… But my mom told me she went to community college in Ohio?" Shiloh questioned, doubt tingeing her voice.

"Your father did not tell you then? About any of it? I had hoped he would at least let you make your own choice when the time was right. Clearly, he has stayed consistent in their cover story if nothing else," she cleared her throat. "I am not surprised to hear about the recruitment letters given your mother's prowess. Not everyone is cut out for the rigor, so it is quite a testament to your potential."

"Did they leave Revned because of me?" Shiloh asked slowly.

"Not at all, my dear. Many faculty live on campus with their families," Margaret replied with a chuckle. "We did everything we could to keep Mariam on, but your father was unfortunately not as gifted and could not have made it in academia. That made the decision for her. She was empathetic, almost to a fault, and deeply loving. Despite her husband's willing sacrifice, she knew he was unhappy, and she could not bear it. She could not bring herself to love her work more than she loved him."

"So they left..." Shiloh said, testing out this new information and trying to map out the implications. "And they pretended psychomanipulation never existed... until she couldn't anymore. Until my mom couldn't anymore."

Margaret nodded, silent but firm.

After several hours, Shiloh stomped down the creaky stairs and into the pouring rain. Margaret had initially displayed a surprising amount of patience, answering each and every question Shiloh had about her mother. Margaret had then attempted to launch into complex theories about the tactics of Draven's dark and twisted mind, but Shiloh just couldn't keep up. None of it made her feel any less lost. If anything, it shined a light on her disturbing knowledge gap.

Her stilted exit may have been rude, she thought as she walked. She hated to let Margaret, her mother's confidante, down, but she could barely keep her eyes open. Barely stand the weight of her limbs any longer.

She fumbled with her key and then, without bothering to change out of her sopping wet clothes, went to the hall closet and gently removed her mother's Tiffany lamp from the top shelf.

She plugged it in next to her bed and the antique paneled glass illuminated, purple flowers and green ivy dancing along the edges of the shade. She fell onto the mattress, mesmerized by the relic of her childhood. This particular possession had been weighted with sadness and rejection since Mariam's disappearance, but the soft glow wrapped around Shiloh like a cocoon. Welcoming sleep to come, she began to drift…

She was a little girl, walking through the woods behind her house in Pennsylvania. Long limbs of her favorite tree, the giant willow, concealed her notch and relief flooded her tiny body upon pushing them aside. It had stayed just as she left it and she climbed in.

Shiloh sat in the leafy cavern below the branches, closing her eyes and breathing in the dewy morning air. In this spot, her world both shrank and expanded. She felt for her journal under the big rock, and began to write, smiling down at her pen. She adored creating and knew her mother would love her latest work. Sometimes the words just flowed, and she couldn't think of a better feeling in the whole world. She wanted to become a poet when she grew up, but that was a secret.

The writing transported her, and a tingling sensation crept into her fingers and toes. Shiloh set her project aside to adjust her position, thinking her limbs must be falling asleep. Something moved in her peripheral vision. Her pen! It floated precariously in the air, all by itself!

Mesmerized, she tried to pluck it down, but the pen flew gently out of the notch, running away from her. Following it, she tried to snatch it again with a little more gusto. It rested just above her head, though, outside the tree branches and out of reach.

Caught up in this strange magic, she failed to notice the other figure until it called her name. Nearly tripping in surprise, Shiloh spun to find herself face to face with a stranger. The young man laughed. He was pale, so pale, but with striking jet-black hair. He smiled softly at her.

"No need to be afraid. I won't hurt you. I'm just admiring the magic."

Despite his warm words, the man's cold, steely gray eyes made her blood icy inside her veins. She had never seen anything like him and without answering, she backed away.

"You know, with your magic you could have anything you want. You could be queen of all the land," he coaxed.

Unsure of herself, Shiloh fell back on fact. She blurted, "There isn't a queen of the United States. Only a president."

"Wow, what a smart girl. How old are you? Six?"

"Seven," Shiloh snapped, insulted at being thought of as a baby.

Hands in the air in mock surrender, the man replied. "Ah, of course. My apologies, I should've known. Do you want to learn more magic? I can show you if you want to come to my house sometime."

She did want to learn. She didn't think she believed in magic, but maybe she thought wrong. She loved to learn new things and was *good* at learning new things. Just as she was about to ask him what he could do, her mother appeared on the path a little distance away.

Her beautiful, kind mother stared straight past him and sternly into Shiloh's eyes, a look normally reserved only for times when Shiloh was in trouble.

Go home, her mother commanded, although not out
aloud. Their special connection. Her mother loved her so
much she didn't even need to speak aloud to communicate
with her. This time, though, the tone wasn't loving. It cut so
sharply that Shiloh forgot her manners and didn't even pause
to say goodbye. She just turned and fled back to the house.

The unpaved path widened before her stumbling feet. The
sky grew noticeably darker, as if someone had taken a bite
out of the sun. Intense dread washed over Shiloh.

She ran.

A downpour enveloped her, melting the trail into a slip-
pery mudslide. The lingering tingling sensation in her fingers
and toes started to build until it felt more like an electric
shock than a sleeping limb. She screamed in pain, incredulity,
and terror.

Beep. Beep. Beep.

Shiloh pressed snooze. A cold sweat drenched her forehead. She lay immobilized by emotion for a long while, trying
to untangle reality from the nightmare. Once her heart rate
had slowed, she rose and changed out of her stiff clothes from
the night before, trying to pull herself together.

A crisp, efficient knock sounded through the apartment.
Shiloh knew that knock. Margaret.

She ignored it and put her earbuds in, cranking up the
volume loudly enough for the pulsating bass to drown out
her thoughts. She let herself get lost in the music and cooked
herself breakfast.

That afternoon, she was both relieved and disappointed
to find Margaret nowhere in sight as she slipped out the door
to check her mail. Before she had even made it halfway there,
though, a purple Mustang coupe barreled up beside her. It
had to be at least fifty years old despite its mint condition.

The window rolled down, and Shiloh rolled her eyes, waiting for the inevitable catcall.

Margaret, barely tall enough to see over the steering wheel, peered out through shades even bigger than her normal glasses. Her small face appeared cartoonish, and despite her anger, Shiloh couldn't help but crack a smile.

"Want a lift, toots?" Margaret grinned.

Shiloh reluctantly circled to the other side of the car and got it. The old cactus was impossible to stay mad at, no matter how unbelievable things seemed to get whenever she got involved. She couldn't tell exactly which parts of their conversation from the night before made her angry versus sad versus confused. This was all so complicated. The world still hadn't reconciled itself the way it always had in the past.

It wasn't really Margaret's fault, but at the same time it absolutely was. All of it. Margaret's love for Mariam shone through crystal clear, though, and Shiloh glimpsed the devoted friend and colleague her mother must have known. If Mariam had trusted Margaret, Shiloh could too.

"I knew if I drove around long enough, I would catch you. I can be patient when absolutely necessary," said Margaret with pride as the car lurched forward. "Have you found any more notes? Had any more dreams?"

"No more notes," Shiloh responded curtly, not yet ready to let Margaret completely off the hook. "I had a strange dream-turned-nightmare about her last night, though. I was little but using psychokinesis, I think. I was sitting in my favorite place in the forest behind our house and then all of a sudden, my pen floated away. A man came and offered to teach me magic, but before he could, my mother found us. I think she used brain-to-brain communication to tell me to go home. Then as I ran home, the sun lost its light, which I don't even think is possible. A horrible darkness came over the whole area and a big shock scared me. Then I woke up."

Margaret cocked her head and let up on the gas pedal ever so slightly, slowing the car to a barely safe speed. "What did the man look like?"

"He had jet black hair and extraordinarily pale skin, like he had never seen the sun. His eyes…" she shuddered. "They made him dreadful. They were the color of ice-cold metal."

"Draven," Margaret whispered. "You have met him then."

"No, I haven't," replied Shiloh, puzzled.

"You just described him perfectly, down to the eyes. Those unsettling eyes. You are sure you did not find another note?"

Shiloh's mouth went dry. She felt her palms clam up. "I'm sure. And none of the events from the other connections had anything to do with me from what I can tell."

Margaret paused to consider. "Yes, true. He seems to be pushing further and further into the realm of what we always considered theoretical brain-to-brain communication. You see, in Draven's previous communications, he infiltrated your mind to tell you a story, show you an experience. From what I can tell, those nightmares were likely memories of his. You were asleep and your guard was down. It seems like this time… no, never mind that is simply impossible."

"What's impossible?" To Shiloh in this moment, it felt like absolutely anything could be possible.

"A false memory."

The idea made Shiloh's limbs weak. *If someone could implant false memories, what else could they manipulate?* Her mind, her place of sanctity now felt dirty and violated.

"But… it felt so real. What if… what if it was my real memory?" Her eyes darted, paranoid and skittish.

Margaret slammed on the brakes and inhaled sharply. "Let us hope that is not the case. If he can access your memories, the consequences could… I cannot bear to think about it right now. We must go see an old friend. He can teach you better than I. Time is of the essence, so there is none to waste."

They fell silent, and her car screamed down the deserted street and back into the parking lot of the complex.

Shiloh followed Margaret into the office but instead of progressing to the stairs, they stopped in front of the wall of keys. Muttering under her breath, Margaret pushed the conveyor belt with her foot, and it began to whir. As it picked up speed, Shiloh's fascination amplified. The belt seemed miles long.

"Why do you have so many keys if you only have seventeen units?" Shiloh ventured, tentatively.

"I need a key to everything," Margaret replied without looking at Shiloh. "Well actually, I do not technically *need* a key… but you know, I have one. It is polite, after all. Revned alone has a whole eighteen feet of keys, and that is just the central campus."

Shiloh shifted her weight back and forth, looking over her shoulder every few seconds—for what, she wasn't sure.

"Ah, yes here! We will go now. Hurry up." Although Shiloh hadn't asked, Margaret added with a wink, "The apartment complex is just a front for my real work." She moved swiftly out the front door and plunged forward in the opposite direction of Shiloh's unit.

"You know, your absolute best and absolute worst trait is your need to explain everything in words. In many cases, words are simply inadequate."

Shiloh couldn't hide her bewilderment at the slight, but Margaret followed up. "Oh, do not be insulted. You know I think you are brilliant. I just mean there is more to this world than you can even imagine. Try not to forget that." Margaret walked past the parked coupe and straight into the unit currently reduced nearly to ruins from the crash.

"Please watch your step. This access station is in less-than-ideal condition for obvious reasons. Those moron students left me with quite a mess to clean up. I had to explain away everything as though it were a common fender bender and not the psychological mess that it was. The authorities here must think I am a real crock." She laughed heartily at this.

"A fender bender? Two men died! That was way more than a *psychological mess* from what I saw."

"Ah, no silly. Those men were not real. We implanted them into the scene—a highly experimental feat by the same Revned professor we are going to see. Unfortunately, for reasons still unknown but now highly suspect, the scene glitched in transfer. That is why you saw the same thing happen twice. Apologies and many thanks for your unwitting participation in the study."

"You mean it wasn't real?"

For once, Margaret appeared to be grasping for words. "It was very real from a psychological perspective. It just did not happen in the physical world. Well, at least the death part did not. Clearly the car's impact did." She paused to gesture at the crumbled brick surrounding them.

"The crowd was comprised entirely of students and other academics. They were trying a new approach to memory implantation—the phenomenon I believe you experienced last night. They did succeed, I suppose, since you apparently believed everything you saw. However, they failed to control the environment, hence the gory details."

Shiloh, remembering Margaret's criticism, accepted the explanation. The cogs in her mind spun double-time, but new and exotic phenomena popped up daily nowadays, so why not?

At that moment, a deep crumbling noise echoed within the half-collapsed space and the smell of wet brick wafted through.

"Drat," muttered Margaret. "Come on, hurry up." She shoved the key into the delicate lock that appeared to have been safeguarding a closet door at one point. "After you. Just keep walking about ten steps or so," Margaret shouted, her voice already fading as if at the opposite end of an extremely long tunnel.

Shiloh entered slowly, cautiously, and tried to work out the innards of this peculiar closet. Enveloped in darkness, her mind sped through her internal stash of physics flip cards. She tried to construct a coherent hypothesis to explain how she could already be seven paces into a three-foot deep closet but came up empty.

Then her world went topsy-turvy. Motion-sickness threatened to get the better of her, and she had to close her eyes momentarily. When she reopened them, she was definitely not at the apartment complex. The sun beat down and her feet touched onto an expansive green field. It appeared to be a central courtyard of sorts, full of people around her age carrying backpacks of all shapes and sizes.

What the hell just happened?

She took a deep breath to prepare her lungs for inquisition mode, but Margaret smacked into the back of her before she could start.

"Ouch!" Margaret yelped, shoving Shiloh from behind, her stick-thin arms surprisingly powerful. "What are you doing standing there like a buffoon? You do not just stand and stare when you get off the bottom of an escalator. Do you?"

"Are we in Narnia or something?" Shiloh's shocked brain still couldn't catch up, and that seemed as likely explanation as any at this point.

"Of course not. We are at Revned," snapped Margaret, looking at Shiloh like she had just flown in from Mars.

"But how…"

"I will explain later. Advanced physics is the premise, though. You should understand it."

On the lawn students threw frisbees, ate snacks, and played music through large speakers. Shiloh smiled, remembering how much she missed her own university days. Unsure what else to do, she conceded to walk at Margaret's heels. They moved rapidly through the main thoroughfare, and Margaret pointed out the various buildings dedicated exclusively to studying the mind.

"That to the left is a psychology building, and to the right is our psychokinesis lab. Coming up ahead you will see the experimental science building. It houses our prized accomplishment, a sleep pod with computers that translate the sleeping person's dreams into videos to be watched later." Margaret's hands flourished in accompaniment to her excited speech.

Nerves buzzing, Shiloh prayed for a more in-depth tour later. They stopped in front of a faculty building with enormous French doors that dwarfed them both. A musty library office, not so different from the apartment leasing office, welcomed them at the top of the stairs. This slowed Shiloh's mind and calmed her just a little bit. Books could always do that for her.

The office appeared to be empty, but as soon as they reached the middle of the room, a racket of yelps and tumbling objects berated them. A boot hung in mid-air at the center of the chaos. Upon closer inspection, a short man with a red scruffy beard was attached to the boot that dangled from an apparently extraordinarily deep bookcase.

"Leonard! How do you do?" Margaret greeted nonchalantly. As he scrambled down, Shiloh couldn't help but notice Margaret's stare lingering a little too long on the stout man's backside.

"Margaret, my dear friend!" exclaimed Leonard, stooping into a kneeling pose. He kissed the older woman's hand, causing Shiloh to blush. "I'm glad you've come so quickly. I can't believe I'm finally meeting Mariam's daughter."

He extended his hand, and Shiloh took the small, chubby fingers in her own as he swept her into an unexpected hug. Unsure how to address him, she stood stiffly and tried desperately to catch Margaret's eye.

"Please, call me Leonard! Margaret's filled me in on your family history and your current unwanted communications. Here you'll be safe. No doubt about that. He shouldn't be able to reach you here because of the electromagnetic barrier shielding the university. It keeps your mind free and clear. Unless of course you are working in a controlled lab environment. My area of expertise is theoretical and practical brain-to-brain connection. I taught your mother many years ago. She was indeed the most promising mind I've met to date. I do suppose it's because of her that we're all here, though…"

Shiloh gulped awkwardly, unsure how to gracefully accept this veiled compliment. Although she enjoyed it, she had never been particularly good at receiving direct praise from strangers. She also did not appreciate that he apparently knew as much about her mother's demise as she did.

Leonard continued to prattle, unbothered by Shiloh's silence.

"We need to sharpen your skills and give you years of knowledge on a tight timeline. It'll be hard work, but I have no doubt that I can do it! Err... I mean we can do it! The lovely Margaret has told me you're already mastering the art of psychokinesis, the foundation for brain-to-brain communication. Quite promising indeed. We'll have to strengthen and control your skillset to start. Once we do that, we need to locate Draven. This is of the utmost importance. The consequences of unchecked psychomanipulation are grave, very grave indeed."

Leonard buzzed around the room while he spoke, pausing only to flourish his arms at the most dramatic points in his speech. His constant state of motion reminded Shiloh of Margaret.

"Unchecked psychomanipulation? That's a new one..." ventured Shiloh.

"That's all you need to know! Psychomanipulation is only one measly idea yet is filled with so many topics. Psychokinesis, brain-to-brain communication application and theory, memory implantation and dream science—all forms of psychomanipulation and that's just the tip of the iceberg, I believe. Actually, as a matter of fact, I know!" he bragged, "Psychomanipulation is the modern term, you probably wouldn't know it if you haven't been immersed in the field."

His exuberance contagious, Shiloh's stomach fluttered with the excitement of it all.

"Obviously," he continued, "this type of power comes with great responsibility and in the wrong hands... Yeek! It gives me the heebie-jeebies just thinking about Draven walking in and out of your mind like a house guest."

This gave Shiloh pause. She hadn't really thought of it that way before but now the seed was planted, and she couldn't push it away.

"I want to learn it all. I want him to go away. And I want to find my mom."

A heavy silence followed as the triad reflected on the loaded statement.

Despite having been on campus for less than an hour, an indescribable sense of belonging washed over Shiloh. She hadn't experienced anything like it since leaving the safety of her hometown in search of a bigger life.

"I'm hopeful you'll be a quick study given your genetics and aptitude for scholarly endeavors." Leonard looked over his glasses approvingly and beckoned her to his desk. "Let's see where you are then. Please open *The Immortality of a Dream, Volume III* to page one hundred and thirty-seven."

"I didn't bring any books." Shiloh frowned.

"No, but I have many. They surround us. You don't need to know the book. You just need to find it and open it using the power of your mind. Elementary stuff, really."

Shiloh took in the challenge and then spun around slowly, trying in vain to find the book with her eyes so she could focus.

"No, no," offered Margaret. "Find your own energy and *then* sense the current of the books. Let the one you seek speak to you and come to you."

Obeying, Shiloh closed her eyes and found the tingle in her limbs. She let herself connect with the room. Initially sensory input overwhelmed her. Soon she started scanning the shelves, slowly at first and then more quickly as she sensed what she needed. A heavy thud crashed behind her as she homed in on her target.

"Oops," she said sheepishly, eying the book splayed on the floor.

"No bother, keep going," Leonard encouraged.

Slowly, shakily, the text levitated and a bumpy journey to the coffee table ensued. Shiloh had to strain her mind, fighting for every inch despite the relaxed state of her muscles. The pages flipped wildly fast and then more slowly until page one hundred and thirty-six quivered. It stood straight up from the spine of the book like a mohawk before falling neatly in place, leaving page one hundred and thirty-seven exposed.

"Marvelous! We'll keep working on your control but given your total lack of formal training or knowledge, this is absolutely remarkable!" exclaimed Leonard. "Try the lamp. I want you to pull the chain off and back on. No cheating and causing an electrical surge, though. With only a week of knowledge under your belt I can hardly believe my eyes."

Shiloh preened. She felt inexplicably fond of Leonard and thrived with the familiarity of academic praise from her new professor. When she directed her energy at the lamp, the chain tugged on demand. *Click.*

The book had served as a warmup and now her energy flowed freely. She tugged the chain on and off several times. Then, to show off a little bit, she moved the lamp right to left without knocking it over. Feeling bold, she then lifted the lamp completely off the end table.

Proudly, she turned to Leonard, but Margaret clapped and rose to her tiptoes in excitement. "Shiloh, wonderful! Let us try direct brain-to-brain. First listen for me, and then repeat back what I say."

Shiloh tried to relax and feel the energy. She tried not to think too hard. She couldn't afford to spoil this the way she ruined everything else by overthinking. In her mind she heard Margaret's voice as clearly as if she were speaking out loud.

Welcome to Revned, Shiloh. You are about to discover a world and a family unlike anything you ever imagined for yourself.

Shiloh smiled, her eyes still closed. How could Margaret know her so well yet barely at all?

CHAPTER 18

Her hair tumbled gently forward, hiding her face as she frowned in concentration. He lurked outside the office, the shadows protecting his voyeurism. He wished he could stay suspended in this moment, watching this beautiful being operate unguarded.

She twirled her dark curls thoughtlessly, allowing herself to be pulled deeper and deeper into her own mind. The office was lit only by a handful of seductive candles. Fire was not permitted in the building after the corner office had mysteriously incinerated. A carelessly abandoned open flame had been the cause. Or so they thought.

When she moved her finger into her mouth… he gasped. Sharp, involuntary desire nearly overpowered his paralyzing shyness.

Startled, she whipped her head up, the spell broken.

"Oh," she squeaked, clearing her throat. "Draven. Hello. Welcome." Her speech sounded stiff and hesitant.

He smiled and entered the chilly yet cozy office.

"Hello, Mariam. I'm so honored to be working with you. I hope you can make my dreams come true." He paused, lapping up her startled reaction. "I mean help me make my dreams come true."

He flushed. "I want to advance the field of brain-to-brain communication. I want to change the world."

At this, she smiled broadly. "Me too. Tell me more."

They drank tea, curled on opposite sides of the couch. As the sun set, their conversation grew in intimacy and fluidity, her brilliance shining through. She never laughed at him, even when he began to share his passion for darkness. He felt like a turtle, belly up, as he exposed his most private work, but the night bolstered him.

"I want to control the variables. I want to expel uncertainty. I want to eradicate evil from the world."

She positively beamed. In this moment, he surrendered. Her light was the only one he did not want to snuff out.

CHAPTER 19

———

Shiloh started going to Revned daily. Margaret had given her a strict lecture on security and then entrusted her with her own key since she wasn't yet good enough at psychokinesis to open doors without one. She dedicated nearly all her time to studying although she still did a little bit of dog-walking. It helped clear her mind and ease the meddling anxiety riddling her thoughts.

Doctoral level courses and private tutoring sessions with Leonard filled her days. She obsessively reviewed notes and made long lists of questions to research or ask her mentors. This habit rewarded her with a rich sense of control. Leonard's nutty professor personality and knack for theatrics propagated further with each passing day, but she had to admit she found it rather charming.

By night, Shiloh cozied up on Margaret's couch with a cup of hot tea as they spoke, chatted even, using brain-to-brain communication. The skill still felt foreign but got easier by the day. Shiloh started to respond without audible words, even though Margaret didn't shy away from commenting on the weakness of her signal.

Shiloh motivated herself by comparing her brain-to-brain development with running. The more she practiced, the easier it got and the longer she could go. She needed the comfort of steady improvement. At night she lay awake thinking about Draven, which inevitably led to memories of her mother. *What if she is alive?* The overwhelming guilt for not going after him right this moment consumed her, gnawing from the inside out.

The rational part of her mind knew she had nowhere near the skill level or strength to find him herself. Margaret and Leonard assured her they had a plan in the works but refused to bring her in. Apparently, it was safer for her not to know, but the exclusion still hit like a punch in the gut. *Why don't they trust me?*

She hadn't encountered any more electrical issues in her apartment until one day she went to rummage for her rain jacket. Flipping the switch, a thin tentacle of dread slithered through her stomach. The closet lit up in quick, erratic bursts as the bulb strobed. Tiny flashes revealed coats and boots leaping up like gremlins coming alive from an underworld.

No. She backed away. She wasn't ready. The thought of him passing her horrible memories felt so much worse than having a simple nightmare. She couldn't stomach the thought of him accessing her brain. Knowing or remembering or whatever it was introduced a new level of intimacy to the interaction. She shuddered, goosebumps crawling up her arms.

She pressed speed dial number three on her phone and Margaret picked up on the first ring.

"What's wrong?"

"How did you… never mind. I need you… There's another bulb," Shiloh sputtered.

The line went dead causing an electric current of fear to weave through her body. Hoping Margaret had hung up and not been cut off in an ominous twist of events, she moved to redial. Before the call went through, Margaret scuttled through the door, breathless.

Side by side, they stared silently at the closet fixture. Curiosity and fear emanated from them both like a bad stench. Shiloh's hands trembled as she unfolded the step stool and climbed onto it.

She unscrewed the bowl of the fixture, and a flurry of papers assaulted her face. Screaming, she ducked and hit her head on the doorframe. Margaret shouted in surprise. The paper fragments lay strewn across the floor and in Shiloh's hair like confetti.

"There must be dozens here!" Margaret exclaimed, regaining her composure. Scooping up a couple, she read aloud. "Only those trusting of darkness understand how connection percolates under its protection. Together, Mariam and I will achieve ultimate control of the human consciousness."

"We will be the gatekeepers…" but before she could finish speaking, Margaret dropped to the floor and started flipping paper notes over like Scrabble tiles. Shiloh bent to help, continuing to read silently. None of them made any sense.

"These aren't confessions like the other notes," ventured Shiloh.

"No, but they might be even more important," replied Margaret.

Shiloh stayed silent, lost in the trenches of her mind.

"There has to be an order!" Margaret's fingers buzzed with motion and excitement as she arranged and rearranged the slips into patterns incomprehensible to Shiloh.

Shiloh's thoughts rewound back to the first note Margaret had read. *Mariam and I. Mariam and I. What did that mean?*

How old were these notes? "Margaret… did Draven ever live here? Was my mother here?"

"This old place? Heavens no! I came here years after they had disappeared mostly because of its powerful electric currents. That is the key to getting nearly anywhere you want to go, you know. I was on a quest, and I wanted to go everywhere."

"Then how did these notes get into the light fixtures? Could he have done that via telekinesis? He talks about my mother, Margaret," Shiloh pressed.

For the first time Margaret froze. "No. That is impossible, even for someone as powerful as he has apparently grown. He could not have planted these notes using psychokinesis or anything like it."

The realization hit them both at the same instant. He had been here. On the premises. In this exact apartment.

Shiloh crumpled into herself, pulling her knees tightly to her chest. "These notes have to be old. Right? Placed before I even moved in, I mean?" Her composure started to unravel, and she raked her hands across her face and through her hair.

"I do not know," Margaret replied, quietly. Her hands shook, wringing each other in slow motion. "To tell you the truth, he has been under the radar, out of the picture, for so long that I was not sure I would ever find him. Obviously, I wanted to know the truth about Mariam, but I was nearly ready to accept the consolation prize of his death. Oh, how I wish I was smart enough to give you the answers." She refused to look at Shiloh and continued to arrange and rearrange the crinkled, dirty notes. Then she stopped, appraising her work. Her face paled a shade. She sat up so Shiloh could see the puzzle via the dim light from the window. With all the mismatched slips of paper, it resembled a ransom note of sorts.

Banish the cruelty of the past.
But let its pain fuel the power of the future.

Light invites attention, visibility, and torment.
Dark yields invisibility, and invisibility yields invincibility.

Only those trusting of darkness understand how connection percolates under its protection.
Only those who embrace darkness harbor any hope of realizing their true power.

Together, Mariam and I will achieve ultimate control of the human consciousness.
We will own the darkness together.
Become the greatest force of all time.
And eliminate the pain people cause each other.

Far too many remain unworthy of the privilege of psycho-manipulation.
Just because a bud grows on a rose bush, that doesn't mean a flower must bloom.
Mariam knows this.
She is my perfection, my equal in every way.

Her light conjoined into my dark.
We will be the gatekeepers of the mind.
With the forest as our salvation, power, and lifeforce.
Stronger than death, we will reign.

This is the foreboding.

"Is it possible?" Shiloh murmured under her breath, afraid to give life to her hope.

"This does not make any sense. Mariam… my friend. She has been gone so, so long," Margaret replied, sounding entranced.

"How long have these been here? When was he here? If she's out there I have to find her," Shiloh set her shoulders back, determined as ever. "We have to rescue her. She needs us." *I need her.*

The pair sat together, caught in their own memories of Mariam. Her laugh. Her smile. Her kindness. Shiloh allowed herself, just for a moment, to imagine a life with her mother. She grappled with the idea of festive family Christmases or summer vacations. Maybe finding Mariam would bring back her father who had retreated so far into himself that she barely knew him at all.

Margaret, as if remembering her role, snapped into action. "We need to keep this, and you, someplace safe. We will bring it to Leonard straight away. Tonight will be most telling if past events are any indication. We need Draven to connect to you while you sleep, but I need to be there to help if he tries any funny business. I have a feeling this is meant to do more than spook us. Come along."

They picked their way through the rubble once again and opened the locked portal door. The weight of the unnecessary antique key made Margaret's shirt pocket sag along with her posture.

"I still don't understand the doors," Shiloh said, trying to distract them both from the note. "They are obviously fantastic and impossible so how can they exist? Is there, like, a tear in the fabric of the space-time continuum or something?"

"That is the right train of thought... I assume your knowledge of The Electric Universe Theory is deeper than you realize, given your area of study. However, I doubt you have ever applied that knowledge to the degree that Leonard will force you to in your studies at Revned," she said, turning up her nose.

"Typical university science departments spread their scholarship and resources so thin they can barely make meaningful progress in any one scientific pursuit. At Revned, we pour everything into proving The Electric Universe Theory. Our school's mission, *Empowering Electric Excellence,* remains at the core of all we do. If we know how electric currents can power the mind, we can understand how they power the world and then the universe."

Shiloh couldn't help but give in to the tiny thrill of new knowledge despite the dire circumstances. She excelled in the technical, scientific world.

"We know, definitively, that the universe's electric currents power our physical and mental realities. No human can do it, but special devices can harness the current and then bend it," Margaret explained. "In fact, I helped to design the first machine of its kind. It is called Bendz."

"Clever," Shiloh conceded with a wry chuckle as she stepped past Margaret's emphatic flourish and through the open closet door.

She had gotten used to the Bendz travel and, thankfully, no longer felt the same motion sickness she had initially. Shiloh, now familiar with the campus, moved hurriedly in the direction of Leonard's office, but Margaret grabbed the back of her shirt and pulled her toward the experimental science building.

"I let him know we were coming. He will meet us at the lab."

Over the past few weeks, Shiloh had asked Leonard about this building on a few occasions, but they'd never had the chance to visit. It looked like something from the future, all shiny walls and cathedral ceilings. Plants draped from a multitude of ledges at varying heights, creating the effect of a gently growing forest. In the fading evening light, barely visible shadows exposed creepy dimensions likely undetectable during the day.

To their right, a set of glass elevators sprang up and down at an alarming rate. Shiloh couldn't see any physical shaft. Instead, tendrils of electricity in wide tubes connected the ten-story ceiling to the top of each vessel. Before Shiloh could fully admire or inquire about the elevators' power source, Margaret marched straight past them to the enormous staircase centered at the opposite end of the atrium.

"Come on. Come on. Elevators are for lazy people as are linguistic contractions. I for one, am trying to stay fit. Body and mind."

Shiloh eyed the woman's five-foot-nothing skeletal frame skeptically and then followed her.

They went up three floors and by the time they arrived, Shiloh was panting like a dog. They stopped in front of a sign that read, "Sleep Pods."

"Sleep Pods?" Shiloh questioned nervously. "I'm claustrophobic. I can't sleep in a pod."

Margaret opened her mouth to reply, but before she could, Leonard banged through the glass door to their left. His arms swept over his head and then extended to the sides as if hugging a giant beach ball.

He never can spare the theatrics.

"Hello, my friends. No time to waste! Come here and show me this note. Or shall we call it a manifesto? We'll examine it under the electron microscope and suss out any patterns than might give us a clue as to where the hell this guy is hiding. Also, oh my *god*! I hear Mariam might be alive? I'm with Shiloh. No *way* is she working with the lunatic by choice."

He continued to babble, asking question after question. Instead of allowing them to answer, though, he inserted his own color commentary. "Come along. Into the lab we go!"

The lab was more elaborate and wonderful than Shiloh could have imagined. She stood awestruck like a child in Willy Wonka's chocolate factory. Leonard, noticing her dropped jaw, smiled and proceeded with the full, albeit extremely expedited tour.

"Here you see the microscopes and the meters. We have volt, ohm, and ampere in all the labs. We obviously have the more obscure units as well in certain spaces. A number of modern descendants of the Bendz machines live here within these cabinets. The compact size really is astonishing. Did you know the lovely Margaret invented the original Bendz? Astounding, really. Remind me to show them to you sometime. Across the way over there are the thinking caps, which fit over the head and project electrical activity and current into vacuum tubes. Very effective for studying. What we need today, though, is this way. The Cadillac pod of the lab—Wonderland!"

Wonderland looked like a massive bunkbed, but with only one mattress. The top "bunk" appeared to be a fragile filament of light that rippled and changed color in random patterns. Around it, the curtain walls stood only half drawn, but it was easy to see how they could pull up on either side to create a private room encompassing the king-size mattress.

"We'll use the combination of Wonderland and a thinking cap to put your dream, or in this case connection, onto a screen. Then we can see and hear what you're seeing and hearing. We can only get minimal detail, but it'll be enough to monitor and keep you safe. We'll intervene as minimally as possible," he paused, grabbing both of Shiloh's shoulders and holding her in front of him like a child. "During this connection, you need to do whatever it takes to figure out where you are."

"Wait, so you're watching my dream, er, I mean connection, if it happens tonight?"

"Precisely!" He fiddled with the microscope, trying to focus it.

"What if it doesn't happen and I have some weird, random dream instead?"

"Oh, don't worry about that. I've *definitely* seen it all. No need to feel self-conscious."

Margaret broke in. "The connection will happen. I have no doubt."

"Wait, what do you mean where I am? Won't I be here?" Shiloh questioned.

"Well… that's complicated. But don't worry about the details. He can't physically take you from here. That's why you are here, after all," Leonard responded nonchalantly.

Shiloh's alarm must have registered on her face because Leonard hurried on before she could ask another question.

"I'm sure we'll have time to analyze everything tonight, so absolutely nothing to worry about, Shiloh dear," Leonard waved his fingers in the air. "We want to get you to sleep as quickly as possible. This should help." He handed her a glass of clear liquid along with a beaker full of a rich auburn colored drink. "Trust me."

Shiloh took a deep, unsteady breath and decided she had no choice. She sniffed and raised her eyebrows. "Water and shot? Isn't it usually beer and a shot?"

Margaret laughed. "No silly, the glass is a powerful sleeping agent that will enrich your neural connections so we can see which parts of your brain are most active during the connection. Do not worry. Hospitals use it all the time. If I know my Leonard, though, that beaker is a shot of something like a Negroni. He is nothing if not superstitious."

Shiloh looked between the two. "Alright, but only because I want to find my mother."

She gulped down the glass of clear liquid followed by the liquor. Almost instantly, her heart rate slowed, and her anxiety melted away. She felt subdued. Relaxed. Zen.

"Here, here let me help you in, my girl," tittered Margaret who had materialized next to her.

"Thank you very much." Shiloh stared in wonder and then smiled and crawled into the extraordinarily comfortable bed.

Margaret tucked her in snugly, which felt oh so nice.

"I love you, Margaret. Thank you for being my friend," she smiled up at the older woman, dazed. Her heart swelled to what must have been three sizes too big. This is what the Grinch must have experienced when he discovered the true meaning of Christmas!

She didn't feel claustrophobic at all.

CHAPTER 20

A subtle tremor traveled down Draven's spine. His yearning to connect with another mind, not through wires but directly, stood second only to his desire to be Mariam's lover. The walls of the sterile, monochrome room seemed to narrow ahead of him, drawing his focus to Mariam seated on the hard, white leather sofa. Eyes closed with the hint of a smile on her lips, she had never looked more beautiful.

He stopped for just a minute to drink in the scene. The final moment before cementing his name and hers together forever in the history books.

She felt his presence, looked at him, and beckoned to the seat across from her on the couch. He basked in her shadow. She took his hands, and he choked nervously before pulling himself together.

Failure was not an option.

They counted down and, just as practiced, simultaneously closed their eyes and centered their focus.

Her words were the brink of a thought, somewhere in his mind just out of reach. He focused harder. Intensified his effort. There. Barely more than a whisper but present all the same.

Hello, Draven were the first words he heard. The first words to ever be spoken via direct brain-to-brain communication. His name from her mind.

Hello, lovely Mariam, he responded.

At this she smiled. He didn't see it; his eyes remained closed. But he felt it.

He knew she was happy, thrilled even, that he was her first. The first. Central to the greatest scientific achievement to date.

Then the spell shattered. Outside the room, muffled cries of celebration rang throughout the building. Brain scan machines resting over Mariam and Draven's heads like pendant lights started to beep and the technicians confirmed that signals had been transmitted and received.

Direct brain-to-brain communication transitioned from theory to practice and paved his path to greatness.

CHAPTER 21

Shiloh drifted, and the canopy of the bed began to light up in streaks of neon. Leonard paced, and Margaret watched intently while biting her nails. Neither knew what to expect.

In her sleep, Shiloh trudged through the dense, lush forest up what felt like an endless mountain. A smattering of shadows camouflaged her footholds, but nevertheless she moved with confidence. The forest had always been her happy place and it didn't scare her. Instead of thinning as she gained altitude, the foliage grew even thicker, snuffing out almost all the natural light.

Ahead, a small, but undeniable beacon of unnatural light filled the empty space left by a snapped branch. She aimed in that direction and kept her breathing steady. *Three counts in, four counts out.*

Within the palatial forest, the artificial illumination felt out of place and her heart skipped with nervous curiosity. As she got closer, she realized the source. A cabin stood about five hundred yards away. She slowed her pace, unsure if she was trespassing. Her eyes searched desperately for any clues to her location.

Shiloh couldn't recall ever seeing a dwelling like this before and stopped to stare. Architecturally the cabin looked simple, but the building mixed mediums and materials she never would have put together for a mountain retreat. The walls and even the roof seemed to be constructed of lightly tinted glass creating an ethereal-looking structure. Steel and wood beams adorned the outside of the house, trimming the edges of the roof and corners of the structure. Unlike most mountain homesites, no trees had been cleared away and massive evergreens hugged the glass walls of the cabin from every direction.

Despite a subconscious feeling of impertinence, she couldn't stop her feet from moving forward. For the first time, she noticed two figures, a man and a woman, crouched over a table. They appeared to be bent over a jigsaw puzzle, heads nearly touching.

The man's pasty white skin glowed under the dim light. The woman faced away from Shiloh, but her shoulder blades protruded unnaturally, and stringy brown hair wrapped her neck. Her quick, angular movements looked robotic in their precision and decisiveness. In contrast, the man moved his pieces at a leisurely pace, seeming to savor every movement.

Dread hit Shiloh like a ton of bricks.

She wanted to stop, crouch behind a tree and just observe, but an invisible force compelled her forward. It paid no mind to the noise she made so her footsteps crunched loudly. She winced, hoping the sound couldn't penetrate the glass of the cabin. She tried to freeze and every few yards her body listened for a second or two, but then her feet relented to the invisible pull and continued on a direct path to the dwelling.

Both mortified and fascinated, she opened the door and a burst of warm air welcomed her cold limbs. A cobblestone floor paved the modest but beautiful room before her. Cozy furniture surrounded an antique wood-burning fireplace, which served as the centerpiece of the living space. A modern kitchen took up most of the front quarter of the cabin. The bed and couch behind it looked upon the oversized dining table where the woman sat hunched over, one knee tucked under her like a child not quite tall enough to sit properly.

Dried roots, leaves, and herbs covered the surface of the furthest wall. A workbench covered in gardening tools and lab equipment stood below the hanging flora. Wilted, drooping plants lay pitifully sliced, dissected, and violated. Even with their insides exposed, most had small petri dishes of water under their roots with just enough liquid to keep them from dying. It reminded her of a torture chamber where prisoners were kept alive only to be experimented on again and again. She shuddered.

She remained silent upon her arrival, but at the sound of the door closing, the man looked up sharply and eyed her like a piece of cake rather than an uninvited intruder.

When their gazes met, Shiloh froze. She would know those eyes anywhere.

Draven.

He smiled and moved around the table, embracing her in a hug. She nearly gagged at the scent of his aftershave. Instead of fighting or pushing him away, that invisible pull tried to tug her arms around him. She used every ounce of her willpower to keep them by her side, though, and refused to hug him back.

"Ah, you made it! Although not as quickly as I'd hoped. I see you've been sharpening your skills. I appreciate that. It's most necessary for someone with your potential. Please stop trying to fight me, though. I have an idea of how this meeting is supposed to go, and it would be ideal if you could stay on script," Draven chastised. He took her arm gently, leading her to a soft armchair in front of the fireplace, and started to remove her wet boots.

"Now, child, I think you recognize me but let me formally introduce myself. My name is Draven Drury. I'm Mariam's soulmate."

Shiloh didn't look at him. Instead, she fixated on the woman at the table.

"Mom?" she turned to him. "Is that her? Is she really here?"

Somewhere deep in her mind, Shiloh could have sworn she heard Margaret's voice encouraging her. *Use your skills,* it said.

She focused all her energy on the back of the woman's head and found the tingle in her limbs, just like she had practiced. Nothing. No threads for her current to latch on to. An invisible barrier sealed the woman away and rendered her mind impenetrable.

Instead, Draven's voice intruded on Shiloh's mind, crisp and clear. *You're in my house. It's rude to leave me out of the conversation. Besides, she doesn't want to talk to you yet.*

He drummed his fingers and returned to speaking aloud. "Your mother and I are in love. More than in love. Despite what your father may or may not have told you, we're connected at the most intimate level. Not just physically, but emotionally. Through our minds."

Shiloh momentarily broke free of the invisible shackles keeping her still and desperately staggered toward the table. The sitting figure still hadn't looked back at her. She needed to confirm that this shell of a woman was her mother.

"Sit back down!" Draven thundered.

Shiloh's legs gave out, forcing her to the floor. But determination set in, and she crawled, desperately grasping for handholds in the stone floor.

"You're spunky. I admire that. But I also thought you were smart, and I'm finding that I may have been sadly mistaken. If you can control yourself long enough, I'll be happy to let you reunite with Mariam. You do something for me, and then I do something for you. You know?"

This gave Shiloh momentary pause. Mind whizzing, she flipped through a myriad of possibilities. Her dismay overshadowed her hope. She wasn't strong enough to fight him, so she had to stand at his mercy and hope he stayed true to his word.

Do not give in, Margaret's faint voice echoed.

Shiloh looked around, trying to calculate her next move. She had to think like a chess master, not a child playing checkers.

"When did you and my mother fall in love?" she asked, focusing hard to keep from tipping her hand.

"Ah, many years ago! Even before you were born. A secret, forbidden romance. Poetic really if you think about it. Rejected time and time again, I pined for her until finally she could deny me no longer. I even visited you, as you may remember from that day in forest. Yes? I did remind you of it not long ago if I recall."

"That was… real?" Shiloh's eyes widened.

"Even nature could feel the weight of my commitment to her." He twiddled his thumbs, and his steel eyes glistened. "It was beautiful. As the storm moved in, she finally professed her desire and I mine. We made love then, in the truest sense of the word. Afterward, we agreed to leave together and meld our minds to each other."

"Meld your minds?"

"Yes. Her incredible belief in the power of good complements my mastery of darkness perfectly. We've been building a way to use our skills together—to pull the strings of the world, so to speak. We've prevented wars and minimized climate change through psychomanipulation. It's not enough, though. The strings are too numerous and our abilities, even combined, too weak. That's why we need you. Your mind, with the right training, could be the missing piece that keeps the world on track."

He walked over to the table and flicked a puzzle piece to the ground. It skidded across the floor and landed near Shiloh's knee. Uncertainty gripped her stomach, and it churned with anxiety as she shifted her gaze back to her mother.

What if I've misunderstood the entire situation?

"You're preventing wars? And climate change? How can you do all that through darkness?" she asked cautiously.

"Control is key. I take away options and control the variables. By extinguishing knowledge of the greedy, horrific choices one could make, only good choices remain." He turned to the table and strode over to Mariam. "Your mother agrees. Don't you, my love?" He stroked her hair but didn't wait for a response. "After all, without my darkness, she might not have made it to this point. She's accomplishing extraordinary things by my side."

Mariam looked up at Draven and then slowly, as if moving through a lagoon, turned around. Shiloh gasped seeing her mother's face for the first time in more than twenty years. Then her heart fell as she took in the gaunt, jaundiced slip of a human. They made eye contact, and despite the woman's battered appearance, Shiloh swelled with love.

"Mom," Shiloh murmured. Without thinking she launched herself off the floor, but before she could get to her destination, her body slammed back against the glass wall with such force it took her breath away.

"No reunions yet. I'm still not sure if you're on our side or not. I wouldn't want you to get her hopes up," Draven scolded, his voice dripping.

"I'm her daughter. She wants to see me!" Shiloh cried. Her anger erupted as she fought to keep tears from spilling over.

"Maybe, but mothers are notoriously unreliable. You remember what happened to my mom. Don't you? From your dream, I mean?"

"What?"

He laughed. "You dug her grave the other night. Or at least I made you think you did. Don't you remember?"

"You killed your own mother?" Shiloh stared, mortified as understanding washed over her.

Draven looked offended. "Of course I didn't kill her. I cleaned up the mess, though. I buried her with my own two hands. My father killed her. He was no good, just like your father, and she was a wild card, just like your mother. One night he broke." His fingers snapped inches from her nose. "And that's exactly my point. It was one of many worst nights of my life. Anyone can snap at any time, but no matter what, the darkness has always protected me. Surely that night it saved my life from the drunken rage of my dad. What happens if the wrong person snaps at the wrong time? That uncertainty makes the world unbearable."

Shiloh's pupils had dilated, and despite her fear, she refused to look away.

"It doesn't have to be this way, though. Don't you see? Science can save us and spare us from heartache and harm.

When I connect the electromagnetic forces between us all…"
He motioned at her and Mariam. "Then tap into the most
expansive botanic network on the planet, my forest, we'll
be unstoppable."

With that, the ground beneath their feet started to shake
like in an earthquake. As pans rattled and puzzle pieces slid
to the floor, Mariam turned away. Shiloh had the odd sensation that thoughts were literally falling out of her mind. She
felt her sense of self slipping away as her physical and mental
strength rapidly deteriorated.

Bile bubbled into her throat before everything went black.

CHAPTER 22

He hadn't slept in thirty-two hours. *Don't stop. Keep going. Just one step further and you'll spur an inevitable scientific revolution.* Biology, physics, cognitive science, neuroscience, and psychokinetics crowded his brain in a poetic chaos. Manically, he flipped pages and mapped notes to thoughts. He couldn't risk the fragile, thin thread of logic by breaking his concentration.

His hand grazed lovingly over a yellowed forestry book. Fond memories of skipping school and hiding deep in the forest with this book resurfaced. It had opened his eyes to the depth of the unseen world. A particularly harsh bully had shoved him to the ground, humiliated him, and this book had offered comfort when no human would.

Electromagnetic fields emitted by trees could be delicate enough to give spiders goosebumps or strong enough to move mountains. He would harness those fields and wield his allies, his trees, to cure the world of its suffering. He could overcome their slow communication speed with the right mathematical calculations. He would connect to them without words, the same way he could with Mariam. He nearly had it if he could just figure out the math.

Then it clicked. The pieces moved into place so obviously he still couldn't believe the approach hadn't been stolen out from under him. He flipped the page of *A Synopsis of the Mind: Physics, Neuroscience, Cognitive Science, and the Interconnectedness of the Psyche* fervently, tearing it in his exhilaration.

He stood so fast that his chair fell over with a clang. The empty library reverberated in appreciation.

The untapped potential before him was so vast he physically pinched himself. Too good to be true. The culmination of his life's work thus far. And it was only the beginning.

This would convince her to stay.

This would make him legendary.

This would give him the power he needed.

CHAPTER 23

Drenched in sweat, Shiloh's piercing scream killed the heavy silence of the lab. She writhed and flailed, frantically searching the area. For what, she didn't know. The world seemed upside down. Leonard rushed to her side, and she shoved him, hard.

"Get away from me. Leave her alone. She's my mother. That's my mother. What have you done to her?" Shiloh cried, hoarse from the effort. It felt like she'd been screaming for a long time.

Finally, Leonard managed to grab her wild arms. "Shh, Shiloh. *Shiloh.* You're fine. Let me help you. You're fine," he repeated the saying like a mantra.

The human contact had the intended effect. Shiloh squinted, adjusting to her surroundings.

"What…" she started slowly before she remembered. *The lab. Revned. Wonderland. Safety.* Looking right and then left, Shiloh tried to clear the haze still coating her thoughts. From her place on the floor, she saw the curtains surrounding the strange sleep pod bed were torn, hanging limply from the rod.

"Did I…"

"Yes, yes. Don't worry about that. We can fix it," Leonard soothed, still talking to her like she was a skittish horse. Then without warning, he hugged her tightly. Fiercely. Protectively. She leaned into his surprising tenderness and hugged him back.

"I'm sorry… It was so real. I mean it *felt* so real," she stammered, trying and failing to adequately portray how the dream had frayed her nerves down to their brittle ends.

"It was real," Leonard whispered assuredly. "I've never seen a connection that strong in all my years of research. The detail on the screen on our end was breathtaking, comparatively, so I can only imagine how it felt to you. Your whole body engaged. Like a sleepwalker. You mirrored here the actions you took in the dream."

She rubbed at her eyes and then touched the throbbing lump forming on the back of her head.

"That happened when Draven threw you against the wall." He nodded at the now bent Wonderland bedframe.

"He has her. A shell of her at least. My mom. I mean Mariam. She didn't even seem to register who I was. He said their minds were melded. What does that even mean?" She paused to take a breath. She needed to organize her questions into coherence, but her brain felt stuck in overdrive trying to fit the pieces together.

"I know. I know. Just take a breath. You're still in shock," Leonard reminded her.

"We have to get her back. We have to save her," Shiloh declared fiercely. The conviction coursing through her body made her feel powerful and purposeful, something she hadn't experienced in a long time.

"It's science beyond its years," Leonard mused. "I don't know how he could possibly generate the electromagnetic current needed to forge, let alone hold, the bond he seems to have with your mother. Are you sure *you* feel alright?"

Shiloh was again struck by his compassion but didn't respond. The information she needed to share with him stirred in her mind but hovered just out of reach.

Leonard waited silently, patiently, studying her with a mix of curiosity and concern.

"I think I know..." she started off, her voice trembling with uncertainty.

"What's your theory?" Leonard pushed, gently anticipating her train of thought.

"Well, we know all living things carry an electric current. Some currents are stronger than others, but regardless it's always there..." she trailed off still nervous. She didn't want to make an idiot of herself in front of him.

Leonard continued to wait, giving her time to process.

She pushed forward. "That includes trees. Right? He referred to the forest as 'his.' And his workbench... Dissected plants covered every inch. They looked alive, but more like mutilated experiments than living creatures. His bookshelf in the glass house was also full of forestry books." She trembled.

Leonard leaned forward and clutched her hand, his grip strong and steady. "Yes, yes. Tell me more. We had visual outlines on our monitors akin to heat maps, but the feed lacks detail," Leonard whispered eagerly.

"Well," Shiloh continued, quickening her pace with confidence. "Trees have currents just like we do. We've just never been able to communicate because our timetables are so different. Currents and signals run so much more slowly through trees than humans that we tend to forget they're responsive creatures. All kinds of compelling theories about how trees breathe, think, hear, and even feel are floating around, but I'm sure you know that. Forests are deeply connected underground through their roots… Under the darkness of the soil a hidden network creates a whole world we never see."

She paused, meeting Leonard's gaze. Her own knowledge puzzled her. She didn't remember learning all that…

"What if Draven figured out how to channel the electromagnetic field generated by the trees? One single tree might not be much, but a whole forest? Low-level current wielded effectively on a massive scale could have huge implications." Shiloh's speech grew rapid with excitement.

Leonard's sharp inhale told her more that any words of assent could have. He seemed, for once, rendered speechless. She felt simultaneously proud and terrified. A tiny part of her had wanted to be wrong.

"I also think he uses the cabin as a superconductor," she pressed. She abandoned caution, and the words tumbled out. "I know glass can't carry a current, but the walls… they quivered like an electric fence."

Leonard's face darkened, and wrinkles Shiloh had never noticed before creased his forehead.

"It fits. It all fits," he muttered, beginning to pace. "If he has that much leverage…"

"He wants me to join him and Mariam's 'side,' whatever that means… He said I have great potential but… Wait, where's Margaret?" Shiloh got to her feet and started walking unsteadily around the lab. Her legs felt like wet noodles, and her body swayed as her head swiveled to scan the space.

"She isn't here," Leonard replied gently.

"What do you mean she isn't here? She needs to know about this," she said, panic rising. She began to march toward the lab's sterile white door.

"She watched the connection, but…" Leonard trailed off as he pointed at the monitors on the opposite wall. "Think about Draven as a computer hacker, entering through a backdoor. The signal from your current was changing color on our screen. You were trying so hard to resist him, but his strength was too much. He used our Mariam to distract you and nearly stole control of your energy. Margaret stopped him."

"Then where is she? Why isn't she here with us?" Shiloh asked, her voice tinny.

"She channeled her own current and the observation technology to interfere with his connection. A risky and forbidden technique, but she didn't even hesitate once we recognized your distress. She was surprisingly successful and severed his connection just long enough for you to escape."

"When everything went black?" Shiloh questioned. "That's the last thing I remember."

"Precisely," he replied. He hesitated, clearly uncertain about what to say next.

"But?" Shiloh prompted.

"But it cost her dearly. After cutting his connection, Margaret collapsed. I believe she had a grand mal seizure, but it's too early to know for sure."

"She's dead?" Shiloh's heart dropped and her world started to liquify as tears sprang to her eyes.

"No, no. At least not for now. The paramedics came and rushed her to the emergency room. You slept through the entire ordeal."

"How could you let me sleep with her in critical condition?" Shiloh couldn't rationalize the level of fury now boiling in her blood.

"You needed to sleep. You were in fragile condition yourself. Your brain had basically just completed an ultra-marathon with only a few miles worth of practice. I couldn't risk waking you too soon. My most trusted comrade went with Margaret."

"Well, Margaret is my only friend," Shiloh snapped. "How could you just abandon her? This *comrade* of yours better be the best damn thing since Eggo waffles."

Eggo waffles? Really?

She couldn't believe the ridiculousness of what she had just said, but under stress she couldn't think of anything cleverer.

"Come on, I'll take you with me to the hospital. I know you two have become remarkably close."

Leonard took Shiloh's hand and, as if leading a frightened puppy on a leash, ushered her into the harshly lit corridors of the academic building. As they weaved through the slick hallways, Shiloh involuntarily compared the smooth bare walls to those of the glass house. This time, the draping plants felt like demons coming to snatch her away, and a shudder coursed through her body.

CHAPTER 24

The canopy of trees overhead knitted his security blanket and collectively breathed in sync with him.

Mariam's sharp eyes burned hot with fury. Why was she so angry with him? His simple psychokinesis had enchanted her little girl. He thought her name was Shiloh, but he couldn't be sure.

He remembered back to before Mariam left Revned so many years ago, he had pleaded, even begged her not to go. Leaving the university meant leaving him, and the idea of losing her felt unfathomable. She had to sense their undeniable bond the same way he did. They had made history together and bound their very souls in the process.

Still, she had chosen that blockhead over him. She married the moron and abandoned their potential. She gave up her greatness and took half of his with her when she left.

Today in the woods, a magnetic force propelled him to meet her. To embrace her. Despite her wriggling, he held her close whispering his love into her ear. She stomped on his foot, grinding it into the ground like an old beer can. The pain scorched his ego.

He found her reserve unbearable. She couldn't do this to him.

He wouldn't give up on her; he would fight. He held her wrists tighter, even as they turned white.

Watch.

He found her current and then that of the trees. Tapping into the tallest one, he joined himself and Mariam to the forest. The surge of power hit like a bump of cocaine. He watched the vastness, freedom, and power of the connection overwhelm her senses. He could see it change her and imagined the feeling, remembering the vividness of his first time as well.

But he maintained control. She did not.

The trees and their invisible network added strength where only weakness had previously lived. He commanded the forest to lift its branches, to shield them from the sun. It obeyed.

The rain poured, as if weeping for him. With him. Then he let go.

Ghostly silence hovered. She looked up at him, wonder and desperation brimming in her eyes. Yearning for another high overpowered all else. He had won.

He cupped her face ever so gently in his pale, callused hands. *Come with me. This feeling never has to end.*

Finally, she conceded.

CHAPTER 25

———

Fluorescent lights beamed down at her from all angles. In contrast to the blackness of the cool autumn morning, Shiloh felt like a bug under a sunlit magnifying glass in the harsh floodlights. She had no idea where to go. She had insisted Leonard drop her off at the entrance of the hospital, yet on her own, overwhelming anxiety crippled her and robbed her of her good sense.

Cautiously, she ventured through the oversized sliding glass doors and into the hospital foyer. Before she could orient herself, a feather-soft touch tapped on her shoulder. She whirled around to an ogre of a woman standing right behind her. The person's massive frame took up a significant portion of the sizable lobby, and Shiloh involuntarily stepped back.

"You must be Shiloh. I can tell just by your energy. Margaret and Leonard have talked so much about you! I feel like I know you." Despite the woman's stature, she addressed Shiloh gently and tilted her head empathetically as she spoke.

Shiloh's mouth gaped open. She stared into the piercing brown eyes that seemed a full two feet above her own. The woman's thick, curly brown hair framed her terra-cotta face and gave her at least another few inches of girth and height.

Snapping her mouth shut, Shiloh tried to decide which question to ask first. This panicked confusion of being the last one to know about anything was starting to get old.

Instead of starting with a sensible question, Shiloh blurted awkwardly, "How are you that tall?" Horrified by her own rudeness, she tried to recover but couldn't put words into the right order. "Margaret, I need to find her. What floor? I mean…"

Kind eyes shining down, the woman gave Shiloh what she likely meant to be a slight nudge toward the elevators. Instead, the decisive shove nearly sent Shiloh reeling. As the elevator rose higher and higher through the floors, Shiloh averted her gaze to the floor in an attempt to avoid any more awkwardness. The silence didn't seem to bother the friendly stranger in the least, but it crushed Shiloh. Grasping for something to break the ice, she noticed the woman's lime green, mud-covered sneakers.

"Nice shoes?" The comment somehow came out as a question.

The giant laughed. "Thank you. They matched my mood yesterday when I got dressed." She frowned, "But I suppose given Margaret's condition, the happy green feels rather inappropriate. I'm Fern. I was the president of Revned University for many years. I envisioned building up that University as my life's work, my legacy if you will." She paused and shrugged. "But I quit so now I get to work with geniuses like Leonard and Margaret daily if I choose."

Shiloh stared, grateful for the momentary distraction. "Why? I mean why did you quit?"

"Running Revned sucked the joy out of me. I remembered my dream. The prestige and the recognition stroked my ego, but the science lit up my life. I love problem-solving and developing new ideas, not being a deferential figurehead," Fern replied, as if they were old friends and confidantes.

The dingy elevator clanged to a stop, and Fern walked out while Shiloh scrambled to follow, still digesting this foreign point of view.

"Where do you work now then?" Shiloh questioned.

Without breaking stride, Fern steered her through a huge set of double doors. "I'm in the theoretical psychokinesis lab. I don't have to calculate any budgets or manage any people. I'm only accountable for myself and my work." She looked at Shiloh. "And my work is pretty freaking cool."

Then, as if reconnecting with the serious situation at hand, Fern rearranged her expression into one of solemn concern. "But none of my work matters right now. What matters is Margaret."

Fern's swift, self-inflicted plunge from the top of the pro-verbial food chain to the bottom stuck in Shiloh's mind. She wasn't sure she should ask but couldn't help herself. "What did people say?" Shiloh queried. "I mean... do they respect your decision?"

Fern frowned. "At first, they started all kinds of rumors meant to peel away a hidden motive for my resignation. Create a scandal. But there simply wasn't one." She stopped and caught Shiloh by the arm. "Through that transition, Margaret stood by me as my most loyal supporter. She never wavered, even for an instant. She's hard to win over, but once you do... she's your ally for life."

"That doesn't surprise me. I know I haven't known Margaret for that long, but it feels like she's my oldest friend."

Shiloh paused. "I do wish I had your confidence, though, even with Margaret on my side."

"Shiloh, you're a grown woman. You can do whatever the hell you want. You know that. Right?" Fern replied carefully.

Shiloh blushed crimson. She knew this on a basic level, of course, but nobody had ever looked her in the eye and endorsed this fact the way Fern just had. Being around so many people who could read her so well with so little context still unnerved her.

Fern continued, "But seriously. You aren't tethered to anyone or anything. Do what you want. It doesn't have to be forever, but don't let everyone else's expectations paralyze you." Then she chuckled. "Obviously that's much easier said than done… It took me many years to figure that out," she ruffled Shiloh's hair, much like one might do to a furry dog.

Shiloh stayed silent, examining this declaration. Many people had told her to "do what makes you happy," but this was the first time she'd actually witnessed someone choosing happiness over prosperity.

She snapped back into the present when Fern stopped short, tugging on the back of her shirt and causing her to bungee backward.

"This is Margaret's room." Fern pointed and strode in without bothering to hold the door for Shiloh.

The low ceiling hovered only inches above Fern's head and amplified the eerie metronome of beeping machines. To Shiloh, Margaret looked asleep. Her frail friend lay on her back, eyes closed, covered neatly by the bedspread. Aside from the machines, the thickly wrapped bandage around her head served as the only indicator of her condition.

Shiloh had to swallow the lump in her throat, her breath catching. She had never seen someone bedridden in the hospital before. Not like this. She cautiously approached to join Fern.

"You know," Fern commented softly. "Evidence shows that the brain of someone in a medically induced coma still hears and processes conversations despite not being able to respond. Let's talk about what to do next. I know all about Draven and your situation."

Skeptical, Shiloh shifted her attention to Fern for a second before training her focus back on Margaret.

Fern continued, "Margaret and Leonard were some of the most promising students I ever mentored. I've been fortunate enough to continue working with them as both colleagues and friends." She paused, voice wavering. "I also mentored Mariam."

Both Shiloh and Fern stayed quiet, reflecting on the very different Mariams they knew.

"Mariam achieved direct brain-to-brain communication before anyone else in the world, you know. Revolutionary stuff, really," said Fern solemnly. "Draven was her communication partner. Smart as a whale that one. Such a shame…"

Fern shook her head, sighing loudly. "I remember it like it was yesterday. The entire campus flooded the green dancing and popping champagne after that first time." Fern allowed a small smile, her eyes still trained on Margaret's comatose form.

That's my mom. She was brilliant. Then she corrected herself. *She is brilliant.*

The faintest trace of a grin haunted Shiloh's face. "I think you mean smart as a whip. Thank you. For saying that, though. I mean about my mom. It means a lot, hearing about her. Sometimes she feels like a stranger now that I know the truth about her younger years."

"Everyone celebrated like they had done it themselves," Fern continued. "Mariam could make you feel that way. Like her achievements were yours as well. She never hoarded the spotlight. She gave credit where credit was due and then some. I think that's what got to Draven's head. He was good, don't get me wrong, but she was the dynamite in that duo. Opposite of her approach, he tended to take far more credit for their work than he ever deserved."

Tears welled in Shiloh's eyes, threatening to spill over. Fern's arm cradled around Shiloh's shoulder. Its length probably could have wrapped around her whole body.

"First and most importantly, we need to keep you safe. Effective immediately, you're enrolled as a full-time student at Revned and will live on campus. Your tuition and housing costs are covered so don't fret about that," said Fern. "Your area of study will be theoretical psychomanipulation. You're not strong enough to fend Draven off on your own, let alone save your mother."

Shiloh jerked her head up, causing her nose to bump up against Fern's oversized bosom. "How did you know?"

"I didn't for sure, but you just confirmed my suspicions. You can't do it alone."

"I can't risk anyone else getting hurt. I'm the one he wants. It has to be me," Shiloh objected stubbornly.

"Agreed," Fern conceded, surprising Shiloh. "You're entitled to play an integral part in her rescue. For some reason, he wants you enough to risk everything by reaching out and contacting you. We need to figure out why you. Until we do, you may be in the gravest danger of us all. I won't let you embark on a suicide mission. Mariam was family here, which means you are too."

Taken aback, Shiloh furrowed her brow. Nobody had ever spoken to her like that, especially within an hour of meeting her. She didn't know a family outside of her deadbeat father, who she hadn't even bothered to contact since her move. She pushed the sting of his indifference away. She didn't have time for that particular emotional spiral.

"I also know you're used to being the smartest and the best at everything you do. It isn't going to be that way at Revned, so you might as well get used to it. You'll be learning with the brightest minds in the world. I believe in your potential, truly, but you have a lot to learn, and this type of learning is very different from the textbooks you memorized at your previous university."

Humbled, Shiloh nodded slowly. She wanted her mother back more than anything. If she had to set aside her ego to do it, she could.

"Well now," Fern turned to Margaret. "How does that sound, my friend?"

The metronome quickened for one beat and Shiloh's eyes widened.

"She agrees," Fern said, appearing satisfied. "She's too weak to communicate via brain-to-brain but even tiny changes in electric impulses have meaning in our world, as I'm sure you're starting to pick up on. Come on, time to get you moved to Revned."

She stalked out of the room with such a heavy lumber that anyone who didn't know Fern might think she was stomping off in a huff. Shiloh scampered after her, still feeling one step behind, literally and figuratively.

* * *

Hustle filled the next few days. Leonard, Fern, and others from the Revned labs came to Shiloh's dank apartment to help her pack. Luckily, she had not yet thrown away all her moving boxes, and they were able to pack up her belongings relatively quickly. They could only a take a few small pieces of furniture, but Shiloh made sure her mother's Tiffany lamp was among them.

Her mind had started to wander, eyes resting on the lamp, when a stack of boxes tackled her from the side. Startled, Shiloh stumbled and looked at the brown tower swaying precariously. Before she could make sense of the phenomenon, two men, skinny as spindles, poked their heads out from behind the boxes.

"So sorry, Miss Shiloh!" one cried. The other fretted, "Are you okay?"

She couldn't help but laugh at their alarm. She had just met this pair today but had already grown fond of them with their tousled hair and impeccable manners.

"Yes, yes." She laughed. "You just startled me, guys!"

They heaved a synchronized sigh of relief. "Thank goodness! We can't seem to get out of our own way, no matter what we do," Wendel lamented, drooping just a tad.

"I'm just so grateful you're here to help. Twelve hours ago, you didn't even know me and now…" Shiloh gestured at the small crowd of helpers. "This. I've never had this much help with anything in my whole life," she shared, a twinge of sadness creeping into her tone.

"Well, that's what friends are for! Fern says family doesn't have an expiration date. Even though we haven't seen Mariam in over twenty years, she'll always be part of the Revned family. Which means you will be too!"

Simon declared, placing a comforting hand on Shiloh's shoulder.

Shiloh smiled her thanks. Moving was so much easier, physically and emotionally, when you had help. Fern's words came back to her in that moment. *You can't do it alone.*

As nice as the intense sense of community felt, it also overwhelmed her. The genuine kindnesses her new friends extended so readily moved and scared her. No questions asked, they showed up. She finally understood the cliche "actions speak louder than words."

Then her mind drifted to the darker aspect of her situation. How could she risk the safety of these wonderful people with her weakness? She acknowledged she had a lot to learn from them but knew ultimately, she needed to shield them. *If Draven wants me, that's what he'll get.*

The parade of boxes and people continued all afternoon until, finally, Shiloh found herself alone. She sat in the middle of her new quarters, a makeshift lab office area turned apartment. The rubber walls of the room reminded her of an institution. The light paint and crooked but bright fixtures Fern had installed herself cast a hopeful light, but Shiloh still couldn't help feeling like a caged animal.

At least I have windows.

After agreeing to the move, Shiloh learned she couldn't live in the normal student quarters because Draven might still reach her there. She needed a space where her own electromagnetic current could remain fully grounded and siloed to cut him off.

Shiloh loved being back on an academic campus despite her less-than-ideal apartment. The musty smell of academia energized her, and wandering the grounds at all hours gave her peace of mind. Although she couldn't completely quell her worries about Margaret, she also couldn't allow herself to wallow. She didn't have time. Besides, worrying wouldn't make Margaret heal any quicker. Or at least that's what she told her pestering anxiety. She had to focus on bringing her mother home. Margaret's self-sacrifice would be worth it, and Shiloh would make sure it never had to happen again.

CHAPTER 26

The thick, delicious night enveloped them away like stowaways. Her doe-eyed, him soaring. Draven knew she couldn't resist him. Couldn't resist the power he promised.

The world was their oyster.

The small suitcase of Mariam's, filled with only a few books, rattled as they drove. He deftly maneuvered the dusty dirt road through the countryside, still high on the moment of her betrothal.

Her words came between long bouts of silence, but when they spilled out, they exploded. She confided in him, outpouring ideas and goals in ways he was sure she had never been able to with her husband.

She vibrated with life, exactly the way he remembered, intentions so pure, potential so great.

The euphoria of he, the student, surpassing the teacher, made every lonely hour studying worth it. Her questions hit like beautiful missiles. He answered them all. Except one.

"Where shall we start?" Mariam whispered.

In this moment, he served as her provider, protector, and leader. He knew he could give her anything she wanted.

"Anywhere," he murmured, fondling her long spider-like fingers between his own.

This response seemed to bewitch her, and she slipped away, retreating into her own mind.

CHAPTER 27

Since her move to Revned, Shiloh had reverted to her "old self" as she had come to think of it. She spent that first early hour of each day reading relevant research publications in bed before making herself breakfast and heading for the academic buildings. She studied, ate, and ran when she could, but not much else. Her swift resignation from the dog-walking company had been poorly received, given her short tenure.

In addition to her class load and special sessions with Leonard, she had begun teaching herself as much as she could from the endless resources at her disposal on campus. She thrived completely immersed in academia, consuming massive amounts of information. Hours passed in the library as she made notes and lists and flip cards, but she hardly noticed.

Now, immersed in an audiobook about the electromagnetic currents in trees, she picked her way through the slick autumn leaves that peppered the sidewalk to the building that housed Leonard's office. Out of nowhere, a hand grabbed her shoulder, and a shadow enveloped her. She yelped, dropping all her books and one ear pod.

No. No… I'm not ready for him yet.

The shadow leapt alongside Shiloh, though, and a deep but feminine yowl echoed between the two narrow buildings.

Relieved but mildly irritated, Shiloh took in Fern's massive silhouette. "You scared the living shit out of me!" she exclaimed, managing to sound only a little cross.

"I could say the same to you, little lady. I see you're still a little bit shaken up. Have you been sleeping better in your new place?" Fern inquired kindly.

Despite the austere feel of the apartment, she hadn't had a single nightmarish connection with Draven since moving in, which, she had to admit, both relieved and unsettled her.

"Yes, yes. I am. Sorry. I didn't mean to bite your head off. I just didn't know you were there. That's all," she replied breathlessly, still not fully composed.

"Come on, let's see how you're doing. By all accounts you've really thrown yourself into your work!" Fern grinned a Cheshire cat-like smile.

"Yeah, Leonard has been spending extra time with me. And Wendel and Simon have generously dived into deep dream science with me," explained Shiloh.

"Ah yes, they're gems. It's my turn to contribute, though. Come on, now. I already told Leonard I'd be stealing you this afternoon. I want to show you something."

Shiloh tried to protest. She didn't have time for detours. Not even a moment should be spared from her precious study hours, but Fern nudged her insistently in the opposite direction she had been traveling.

Shiloh had filed Fern away as a kind ally but not a real resource. It wasn't that Fern didn't know what she was doing, her approaches were just so… old school. From what Shiloh had heard on campus, Fern preferred to live in the stone ages of psychomanipulation and the new and cutting-edge science didn't have a place in her labs.

On the other hand, Fern had been extraordinarily kind to her, and Shiloh couldn't work out how to decline politely before getting whisked away. So off she went to Fern's stone cottage on the edge of the Revned grounds. Trees camouflaged the residence and gave it a certain privacy from the hustle and bustle of student life. Shiloh found this ironic, given Fern's name.

"So," Shiloh started awkwardly. "How long have you lived here?"

"Oh wow! I think it has been about fifty years," Fern replied, her tone suggesting more of a question than an answer.

Shiloh nearly stopped in her tracks. Fern didn't look a day over forty, let alone living in this specific house for over fifty years.

"Yes, that is about right. I was twenty-five when I moved in. Right out of grad school," Fern continued to muse.

"You're seventy-five?" Shiloh blurted out before she could stop herself. She clapped her hand over her mouth attempting to undo her faux pas. Flustered, she tried again, "I just mean… you just… you don't seem that old."

Well, I tried.

At this, Fern bellowed out a laugh. It reminded Shiloh of Margaret's laugh only a few octaves lower. "I believe you've been told before that things are not always as they appear. Am I correct?"

Shiloh reflected back to one of her first encounters with Margaret and sighed. "Yes, but I can't help it. My brain is two steps ahead of me sometimes. It's like jumping to conclusions is a bad habit."

"It absolutely is!" Fern agreed. "You really need to get that under control if you want to be successful in this quest."

The ground softened underfoot as the two crossed the dewy grass outside the cottage. Despite the undeniable incongruency between the tiny dwelling and Fern's nearly seven-foot stature, the home somehow fit her perfectly.

"Let's talk about that over tea." Fern guided Shiloh into the cozy cottage.

Inside, floor-to-ceiling floating shelves lined the walls. Instead of the books Shiloh had grown accustomed to seeing on Margaret's shelves, these burst with small, meticulously labeled glass bottles containing exactly one organic specimen each. Fern's collection didn't seem to have any theme or organization to it, and Shiloh could see everything from blades of grass and animal hair to hot pink gas in clustered groupings.

The array of specimens drew Shiloh in, and she wandered over, fascinated. Relying on back-of-the-napkin math, she calculated there must be hundreds, if not thousands, of bottles here.

Fern walked up behind her holding, of all things, a turtle. "Shiloh meet Jigsaw. He's been my partner in crime for the past twenty years. My buddy," she praised, kissing his green, scaly head.

"Hi there, Jigsaw." Shiloh reached out to pet his head with one finger but as she got close, he snapped at her. She jerked her hand away. "Jeez!"

"Oh yeah, sorry. He's sour as kumquat with strangers." Fern then proudly started to explain the organization system of the jars. Maybe it made sense in Fern's head, but the methodology sounded completely nonsensical to Shiloh and left her thoroughly confused.

"But *why* do you have all of these? Dead things can't carry current." She paused for a beat. "Right?"

"Not right… But that's a lesson for another day. It's not the state after death I'm interested in although I do dabble," Fern explained. "It's the right-before-death experience. That's the topic I study."

"What about it?" Shiloh frowned, trying to predict the answer.

"Well, as you probably already know, when people become close to death, an electromagnetic disturbance occurs. This is most well-documented in horror films. You see the lights flicker before the massacre or the candle snuff out at the precise moment a person's heart stops. Right?"

Shiloh had never given these phenomena a second thought. She'd always assumed them to be overdramatic theatrics.

"You of course know all about scientific forces—nuclear, gravitational, and electromagnetic. Well, I believe death is another fundamental natural force. Most people think it's impossible for death to be responsible for electro-conduction, but I disagree. I hypothesize that death is the ultimate super conductor."

"How can death be a conductor? It's not a substance," Shiloh countered.

"Are you sure about that? I've nearly proven it." Fern's eyes glimmered.

Death as a force instead of a state. If death is dynamic, rather than static… Even Shiloh, with her limited knowledge, could see how revolutionary the discovery could be. She stayed silent, waiting for Fern to elaborate. Instead, the older woman basked in the silence.

"Do you think your work can help us get my mom back?" Shiloh finally inquired.

Fern considered her response carefully before responding. "I do. But it'll take time."

Shiloh blanched.

"Remember, you and Mariam have both made it this long. Another few months or years won't kill you, in all likelihood."

"Years!" Shiloh exclaimed. "You've got to be kidding. We can't leave her there for *years!*" She tried and failed to control her facial expressions, rolling her eyes.

Fern didn't get it.

"I don't have that kind of time," Shiloh continued. "You know that. He could hurt her at any moment, especially if he can't find me. He's probably already figured out I'm not in my old apartment anymore."

Fern frowned. "How long has your mom been gone now? Twenty years? I can't imagine how you must be feeling, but you need to let us help you. You have so much to learn, and he might be the most powerful mind in the world. You can't rush this. *That* will certainly kill you."

Shiloh nibbled her lip, biting back her rebuttal. She hadn't expected Fern to underestimate and baby her just like everyone else. She would prove them all wrong. She'd double-down her efforts and rescue her mother before anyone else got hurt. A plan started baking in her mind, and for a moment, her thoughts swept her away.

Turning back to Fern, she asked, "How do you measure death as a force?"

At this, Fern launched into an explanation of her unique, and from what Shiloh understood, proprietary "Current Counter" device. She designed it to trigger at the exact moment of passing, capturing a snapshot of the electromagnetic fields in the area where the death occurred."

"So… you kill things?" Shiloh quickly followed up. "I mean animals and plants?"

"Yes, exactly! I love nature more than the average bear. I even compost out back. But in the name of science, I must cover uncharted territory! We have to go back to the roots of life, to harness the purest and most powerful connections. All the machinery these modern scientists use takes away the purity of the craft." Fern turned and started to traipse heavily across the cottage toward the kitchen, the bottles on the shelves clinking like a disheveled wind chime in response. Halfway across the room, she spun around, catching Shiloh off guard. "When I stepped out of the spotlight of Revned leadership and truly dedicated myself to my mind, I realized the void I was trying to fill wasn't just in my heart. It was physical."

"Okay…" Shiloh responded, unsure where this sudden change of subject was going.

"My body felt fatigued, and my joints ached all the time. No matter how much down time I had, I could never get ahead, but when I spent time in the forest, at the beach, or in the meadows, the most curious thing happened. My aches went away, and my energy level buzzed. I spent my time exploring, hiking, camping, and otherwise traversing the Earth without the aid or impediment of any technology. It felt so odd to be utterly disconnected yet…"

Shiloh waited, captivated. She knew the thrill of being disconnected the way Fern talked about now.

"That's where it started. Just a jolt here when a branch snapped or a twinge there when I accidentally stepped on a bug. But I couldn't deny it. When I really tuned in, I felt the energy and opened my eyes to the vastness and the possibilities of the undiscovered." Fern turned to Shiloh and swept a passionate hand across a small shelf, sending glass jars flying and shattering against the far wall.

"It's become my life's mission to rebuild the long-forgotten bridge between humans and the rest of the natural world. For years, I've worked to find a way to truly communicate. And I'm so close. I can feel it. I crave the understanding of both life and death. I have to know how it all fits together."

Fern's frenzied gesturing had turned into aggressive pacing. Shiloh's own feet shuffled uncomfortably, and she took a few steps back to hide her impatience. The thought of Fern's fervor escalating and sending more bottles flying caused her to retreat one more step. This all sounded a little hippie and possibly a lot manic. She needed a scientific genius, not a nature freak, if she was going to get her mom back.

CHAPTER 28

The drive stretched out, hours upon hours, but time with Mariam would never feel too long. His unlimited access to her gave him the visibility into her habits and inner workings he had only ever fantasized about.

They drove for fourteen hours that first night. Through the rolling, rural landscapes, they meandered on the winding small town roads and traversed the city streets of the Midwest.

Finally, he could drive no longer. They pulled off into the forests of Voyageurs National Park and found a secluded, private spot to camp. She begged him for a connection like they had before they left, and he reveled in her longing.

He took his time setting up their campsite, keeping one eye on her, drinking in the push and pull of her discomfort and desire. Alas, he could not make the poor creature wait any longer. The tips of her current reached into his mind, tickling the senses that had been dormant for so long.

He took her hands in his and begged. *Wait.*

This delicate, intimate form of communication drew them dangerously close. He channeled his trees, his friends as he had come to think of them, and then he penetrated her mind.

The feeling never got stale, he knew. He writhed in anticipation of the moment she felt it.

It didn't disappoint.

He watched the wonderous, overwhelming sense of being alive spark every cell in her body. He was used to the sensation but could appreciate the novelty for Mariam and enjoyed nothing more than watching this orgasm of the mind.

As was he, she was powerless to stop the lust that followed this unrivaled connection with the world. She recovered her faculties slightly quicker this time, but when he let go of her, she looked up at him and clasped his hands again. The same wonder as that first time filled her eyes.

You made the right choice, he encouraged as her hands filled his palms with warmth. *Your skill, your mind, was wasting away, rotting and decomposing. But now you can be who you were meant to be.*

She looked away, gazing into the setting sun. "I know," she whispered aloud. "Every day felt like drawing out an inevitable failure. I thought my family was enough. I thought I could be happy…"

A tear trickled down her face. "But I need this. I need to be more. I can't betray myself for the ones I love anymore."

CHAPTER 29

Light streamed in through the dining hall window to Shiloh's left. Although the expansive space felt more like a concert hall than a cafeteria with its sixteen-foot stone ceilings and stained-glass art, Shiloh found it comforting rather than intimidating and basked in the mid-morning bustle. Wendel and Simon sat across from her holding hands and engaged in a respectful but spirited debate about whether different current strengths and paths could actually influence whether you had a dream or a nightmare.

Shiloh had been interested in the topic and grateful for the distraction, but her mind kept drifting. Ever since the visit to Fern's cottage, the implications of death as a source of energy scrolled through her head. Although it hadn't been stated aloud, Shiloh understood that Fern's research was confidential.

She recognized the groundbreaking nature of the discovery, and it was killing her that she couldn't quite link it to her mission yet. She'd racked her brain for scraps of unused knowledge Leonard might have shared in one of their lessons and even started rereading a few key texts with a critical lens.

New searches of the vast library archives at Revned stretched for hours at a time. Still nothing.

"Okay, Shiloh, you're the tie-break. What do you think?" asked Wendel.

She blinked a few times and looked at the spindly pair. She grinned sheepishly, no idea how to answer the question.

"Sorry, I was living in my head for a minute. What am I tie-breaking?"

Simon palmed his hand to his forehead.

"Never mind, never mind," Wendel, the grumpier of the two, muttered. "You can't tie-break without context."

Shiloh attempted reconciliation with her best smile. "Sorry, guys. I'll do better tomorrow. I promise. I need to head out, though. I'm going to visit Margaret. They think she'll be ready to wake up any day now."

They waved their goodbyes, and she hurried to the bus station, just barely catching the old heap of metal before it sputtered away. Clearly Revned did not place the same emphasis on updating infrastructure as it did on updating labs.

Shiloh bounced every time the bus hit a pothole and the torn seat cover kept catching on her jacket. Mild car sickness had started to kick in. When the bus finally got within a few blocks of the hospital, she jumped off and walked the rest of the way. It would do her good to clear her mind before talking to Margaret anyway.

Upon entering the hospital room, Shiloh saw the heavy gauze had been removed from Margaret's head. In its place, only a few stitches poked out from beneath a butterfly bandage.

That's a relief.

"Hi, Margaret! You're looking well today. Ready to wake up maybe?" she asked hopefully as she pulled up a chair. More softly, she added, "I miss you."

The monitor next to her beeped in response. Frowning, Shiloh took hold of Margaret's hand. Her friend had to be in there somewhere.

Then, as if in response to her thought, Shiloh felt the slightest tendril of a tingle in her hand and a whisper in her mind. *Shiloh, you silly girl. I will be up in no time.*

She could hardly believe it. Almost as if in reflex, she cried. "Margaret!"

Margaret's voice chastised. *No! Brain-to-brain only. You must keep your skills strong.*

Shiloh didn't even mind the scolding. Her confidante was back! She launched into a long-winded explanation of her connection with Draven, the move, and even Fern's confidential research. She pushed aside the inklings of guilt threatening her conscience about that last revelation.

Margaret's voice stayed silent for a long while. Shiloh thought her friend must have fallen asleep, but as she shifted to move the chair back, Margaret's voice rang out in her mind. *I knew the nature of Fern's work, but not all the details. It sounds like she is much closer to proving her theory than I had imagined. We must use it to our advantage. If Draven is using the trees, we have to tap into another, more powerful force.*

Then silence. Shiloh felt bad for exhausting her fragile friend. The deep breathing of sleep soon ebbed and flowed from Margaret's body, and Shiloh reluctantly got up to leave.

She appreciated Margaret's words but needed more. She yearned for a simple textbook of formulas to memorize and tell her what to do. She could succeed if someone just told her what to do.

Then she had an idea.

Shiloh rushed home, enduring the bus ride while impatiently tapping her toe. She busily wrote down the new plan for the rest of her day in her tattered purple planner.

The bus hadn't even come to a complete stop when she jumped off, the fall wind whipping her hair into her eyes. She raced to her makeshift apartment and dug out the old textbooks from her undergrad days. She gave her favorite a quick hug to her chest before dumping it into her backpack alongside her Revned books. She took the haul to her usual room in the library and locked the door behind her, heart pounding. The whiteboard wall in front of her loomed, as if to challenge her very presence.

Time to get to work.

The flaking walls and stained carpet offered little inspiration in the stuffy, windowless workroom. Even so, her task consumed her, and time became irrelevant. She worked feverishly, unwilling to stop even for a moment as the minutes and then hours ticked by. Her best ideas came in spurts. She knew this about herself. She was so close. It felt too good to be true. The solution couldn't be this simple. Or could it be? Had she just been overthinking it?

She reworked the equation over and over, first as a physicist, then a cognitive scientist, and then a naturalist. It all fit. She still didn't believe it, though. If Fern hadn't been able to draw conclusive conclusions, who was she to figure it out? She had to test her hypothesis.

She snapped out of her trance, bladder ready to burst, and looked up at the grimy wall clock. She needed a break. Reluctantly, she stood and exited her little cave, emerging into the narrow hallway and closing the door behind her. The library was pitch black to her bemusement and only the emergency exit lights loomed overhead. The darkness outside felt oppressive and suffocating. Even though she loved the library, she had to admit, alone in the dark it gave her the creeps.

As she picked her way through the dark stacks to the restroom, the lights flickered. She froze, absorbing her surroundings, but saw nothing unusual. Heart pounding, she scurried to wash her hands and get back to the relative safety of her study room.

When she emerged from the bathroom, the library remained still and silent, but then, without warning, every light in the building illuminated. Every computer, printer, and projector vroomed to life in unison. The tingling energy started in her fingertips, but the feeling quickly spread and the whole of her physical being buzzed. Her mind raced much too fast, and a strange sensation washed over her. It unsettled her but also gave her a sense of peace.

Then she felt so happy, like she was floating in the clouds without a care in the world. The library transformed into the most wonderous place in the world, where possibilities remained steadfastly endless. She marveled and relaxed, smiling as she pressed her nose and fingertips to the cool glass of the floor-to-ceiling window overlooking the campus. She stared lovingly into the beautiful grove of aspen trees outside. Her emotions pulsed in a way she had never experienced.

But wait.

What is happening? Why are the lights on? This isn't right.

The familiar paranoia crept in, curling itself around the edges of her consciousness; barely perceptible but present all the same.

Then a voice echoed, in her head. *Shiloh, my girl, my baby.* Mariam prodded softly, nudging Shiloh's anxiety aside. *We need you. I know you think he's bad, but it's not true. He's my intellectual soulmate. Come join us, my love. You can be happy forever. You can feel just like you do now all the time. Happy. Safe. Fulfilled.*

Shiloh couldn't make sense of the words. Her thoughts swam, trying to diverge in a million different directions all at once. Her body, almost numb at this point, had stopped taking commands from her brain, and her arms hung like wet noodles.

Focusing as hard as she could, Shiloh managed to reply. *Mom. Mom, are you alright? I'll save you. Don't worry.* She gasped back the sob swelling in her throat before continuing. *I've missed you so, so much. I'm so sorry.*

Mariam's voice rose an octave. *Don't say that, Shiloh, my love. I'm the one who needs to apologize. I left you as a mother never should. But you have to understand. I was so stifled and so deeply depressed, failing as both a mother and a scientist. By leaving, at least I could be successful in one of those disciplines. I tried to give you a gift in relieving you from my burdensome sadness.*

Shiloh couldn't hold it in any longer and began to cry. *I missed you so much. How could you leave me? How could you leave us?*

A long silence followed, and the tingling sensation started to fade. Desperate, Shiloh stretched out for her mother, her mind flexing as hard as it could. *Stop, don't leave me! I can't lose you. Where are you? Why do you need me? I'll come to you. Just don't leave,* she begged through her tears.

Mariam's voice returned ever so faintly. *Meet me in the clearing behind Fern's house. Friday at dusk. I need you. I need you. I need you…*

Shiloh could barely perceive this last statement. It sounded as if her mother's voice was drowning.

The lights flickered out. Shiloh lost her last semblance of composure and with it her ability to use brain-to-brain communication.

"No! Come back! Mom!" she screamed, her horror piercing the library's silence. All at once, the floating sensation stopped and the atrium began to spin as her mood crashed. The dark heaviness crushed her soul as the high was snipped away. She wished she was dead. She crumpled to the floor.

CHAPTER 30

He could hardly contain his excitement. Mariam would love it.

The trees loomed, paving the dirt road in front of them with ghoulish shadows. The tinted glass roof of the structure peeked through, teasing him with the veiled exposure.

As they approached, he drank in the ideas that bubbled from her like boiling water overflowing from a pot. He couldn't believe she was the same woman he had begged for so many years to come back to him. Back to their work together. The hot shame of her initial rejections still crawled up his spine when he thought about them.

He knew her misery. That confining depression could slowly eek the life from you if you let it. Her intelligence could not be smothered, and her desperation for relief from the mundane worked to his advantage. He had explained the connection to the trees to her... partially. He couldn't trust her with all of it. Not yet.

When he stopped the car, she inhaled sharply, as if coming up for air after a long dive in the ocean.

"I've never seen anything like it," she breathed.

"That's because there is nothing else like it." He opened the passenger door and gestured for her to follow him up to the door. "I've spent the years since my departure from Revned building it. For us. This is our home. We don't need to worry about privacy. I own ten acres of land in every direction," he smirked, unable to keep the pride from his voice.

"The walls are constructed from glass infused with tiny particles of silver."

Mariam paused to digest. "So the home is conductive in of itself?"

"Yes, and it's connected to the root system of the surrounding forest. As long as you're inside, you can leverage the electromagnetic currents of the forest all the time without needing to consciously connect to them as we have done thus far."

"That feeling…" she started.

"It'll never go away if you're in the house. It comes from the extreme current. The extra stimulation of your limbic system elevates your dopamine levels."

Her eyes widened. "It's just that… I feel like myself again when I'm connected with the trees. My depression is just… gone."

Hesitantly, she pushed the door open and walked in.

He followed behind, observing as her shoulders instantly relaxed and that beautiful, soft smile she wore so well took residence upon her luminous face.

Together they lay on the rug and watched the trees melt silently into blackness. The stars speckling the quilted night sky became the only beacons of light for miles.

CHAPTER 31

Shiloh sensed a presence. Her head spun, and her limbs ached, like she had been run over by a train. A blinding fluorescence beamed down into her eyes, sending hot streaks of pain through her temples.

Why is it so bright?

A cloud moved in to block the harsh light, and Shiloh squinted. Fern's curly hair, not a cloud, hovered above. Confused, Shiloh tried to sit up, but the motion made her queasy.

"Shiloh? Shiloh!" Fern grabbed her shoulders and shook her like a ragdoll. "Good gracious what happened? Have you been here all night?" Turning away she yelled into the small gathering forming around them. "Someone call a doctor!"

One frightened-looking student who had to be a freshman, started to scuttle away, presumably to obey Fern's order, but smacked right into an elderly gentleman moving in their direction. The man grunted in annoyance but continued to shuffle to Fern and Shiloh.

"No need, no need," he mumbled.

"Arthur! Thank goodness. I don't know what happened. I found her just *lying* here! She doesn't have any visible injuries but she's so out of it I don't want to take her home without a proper exam," Fern blurted, lacking her normal levelheadedness.

Arthur, with great effort and the assistance of Fern's sizable arm, lowered himself to the floor and pushed his enormous glasses up his nose. "Well then, let's take a look. No use turning our respectable library into a circus over nothing."

The doctor took his time measuring Shiloh's pulse and taking her temperature. She recoiled, the stench of his stale coffee breath increasing her nausea. Seemingly out of the folds of his wrinkles, he produced a small flashlight and shined it in her dazed eyes.

She winced and looked away. "Why are you doing that?" she croaked, throat still hoarse from sobbing the night before.

"Young lady," he dropped his voice to a whisper. "I suggest you go lighter on the party favors next time. Especially if you plan to come to a distinguished scholarly haven such as this library." Curtly, he rose from the floor and turned to leave. He walked away slowly, pausing only to announce that Shiloh would be perfectly fine after a glass of water and some ibuprofen.

She blushed and averted her eyes, trying to make herself as small as possible. Whispers and snickers from the crowd circulated as Fern scooped Shiloh up into her arms as easily as if she were a toddler. The large woman cradled Shiloh and strode out of the library straight for her cottage without saying a word.

After placing Shiloh on the couch and bringing her a glass of water and a puke green, nonuniformly shaped capsule, Fern studied her charge. "I refuse to put something as toxic as ibuprofen in your system, even if I might be mad at you. My natural capsules offer far more efficient and effective relief anyway. I make them myself by hand."

"That explains a lot," Shiloh replied, looking hesitantly at the pill.

"Well, out with it then. What the hell happened last night?"

Shiloh gulped, unsure whether to reveal the truth or keep it to herself. She knew she would likely be locked away "for her own safety" if she told Fern the truth. "I don't exactly know," she started, dodging the question to hopefully buy a little bit of time.

"What were you thinking? I would've never imagined you to be so irresponsible. Alcohol? Drugs? Both? I know this has been hard on you but my heavens, we all want to help if you just let us."

"How exactly are you planning to help?" Shiloh exploded, unable to stop herself. "You think I'm too stupid to understand your work even though it's probably the key to getting my mother back, and instead of teaching me about it, you spend all your time being one with nature. I'm killing myself to find answers, if you haven't noticed. I know you think we have time, but we don't! You just don't understand. I was in the library all night working through my own theory, and I think it actually might work!"

Fern looked simultaneously bewildered, startled, and speechless. She got up and walked to the window, staring out at the thick forest, her usually Zen demeanor stiffening just a fraction. Shiloh sank deeper into the sofa, crossing her arms tightly across her body. She knew she must look like a sullen child, but she couldn't help it.

After what felt like an eternity, Fern spoke slowly, still facing the window. "Tell me your theory."

Shiloh launched into it, refusing to give way to her self-conscious demons telling her to shut up. Through a combination of her applied physics knowledge and the cognitive science and theoretical psychomanipulation she had been learning at Revned, she told Fern she thought she had worked out a way to tap into and harness the energy of the animals in the forest, similarly to how Draven might be using the trees.

As she spoke, Shiloh could almost see the cogs of Fern's mind spinning. Occasionally, Fern would stop to ask questions, reverting to professor mode. "How do you account for the space between animals? You'd need to make hundreds or even thousands of individual connections to reach each and every animal. That's way too many for even the strongest minds to maintain at any given time."

"Not if you can ensure a proper chain reaction," Shiloh replied. "If each connection cascades to only one more organism, the reaction could be sustained as long as the integrity of the chain remains."

Fern's eyes widened. "But how? The math…"

"I've done the math," said Shiloh. "I think."

Natural pain relief capsule having kicked in, Shiloh felt much better, and she and Fern scurried back to the library. Luckily, Shiloh's workroom remained undisturbed. Together they studied the board, not speaking for a long time.

Fern took out her paper, pen poised. "Walk me through it."

Shiloh took a dry erase marker and furiously scribbled on the whiteboard wall, showing the steps of her mathematical calculations. An hour later, she beamed, pride swelling. Her biggest pleasure in life was proving people wrong when they told her she couldn't do something.

Fern stroked her chin and then pointed to the board, her tone sober. "The middle section." She walked up and tapped it. "Doesn't work. You can't apply Newton's Laws of Motion and Einstein's Theory of Mass Energy Equivalence to bridge logical leaps regarding psychomanipulation."

"Why not? They're scientific laws," Shiloh retorted, frustrated and embarrassed.

"They're antiquated and outdated in this application," Fern explained, coming over to hug Shiloh. Then her voice softened. "You know, you can't always be right. If you're anything like me, which I suspect you are, the amount of pressure you're putting on yourself borders manic. But it's not helpful. You aren't going to be able to force this. This has been my life's work. I've done more equations and spent more sleepless nights than you can imagine trying to make these principles work together, but they just don't. I'm sorry. I want to find her more than anything too, but you can't expect to learn everything all at once."

Shiloh's face had crumpled into a sad, angry facade. She averted her eyes, consciously willing herself to think about new items to add to her list of research topics instead of bursting into tears. Anything to distract her from Fern's concerned gaze. She hated crying in front of people. She tried to push away the lingering guilt about the half-truth with which she was stringing Fern along. She still hadn't mentioned the connection with her mother.

Shoulders slumping, she turned back to the faulty math. "Why did you let me blabber on for an hour if you knew I was going to be wrong?" Shiloh asked, annoyed.

"Because you needed someone to listen," Fern replied simply.

Shiloh let the silence hang between them, waiting for more but it soon became apparent that was all. "But I wasted your afternoon," she prodded.

"I don't see it that way. I'm here to teach you. Sometimes that means imparting knowledge, but other times it means listening, supporting, and learning the world from your point of view."

Shiloh wasn't sure how to respond. None of her physics professors had ever taken that approach.

"Now, though, I'll revert to the traditional method of teaching," Fern said, snapping her fingers as if performing a magic trick. "First, we need to make sure your foundational psychomanipulation is rock solid. Then we'll venture into communication with the natural world. I'm going to teach you everything I know. We'll save her but we have to be smart about it."

Fern wrapped her arm around both of Shiloh's shoulders and steered her out of the library toward the cottage. "We have some long nights ahead of us, my friend."

CHAPTER 32

It had been seventy-three days, three hours, and fourteen minutes since Draven had arrived in the forest and rescued her from her suffocatingly depressing life. Since she had last seen her young daughter. Since she had last held the aroma of her homemade soaps in her nostrils. Since she had freed her family from herself.

Mariam felt so damn *happy* as she rode a high comparable only to the first time she had ever connected to another human mind. Draven's mind. She had been chasing that high ever since.

Then he had delivered it to her all at once, all the time. Pulling her out of the depths of her rock bottom, he had shoved her into the light and shown her that the world she had so desired still existed. It wasn't a fairytale but real.

They could connect to this Earth in ways she had only ever fantasized about.

She spent her days pouring over published texts and drafting some of her own. His companionship nudged her along. It was so easy, just the two of them. Scholars by day… but what by night?

He became more tempting as time passed, like forbidden fruit just out of reach. Her mind told her no, but her body started crumbling to the pressure of his advances. She thought she had moved past this stage in her life, but as she unpeeled the layers of this complicated being, longing pressed into discomfort.

He wasn't her husband; not gentle, nor kind, nor easy-going, but his brilliance and enthusiasm captivated her. A lifetime of mistreatment had left him scarred and misunderstood. How wonderful it felt to be the object of such passionate affection. His mind and his dedication to their cause enthralled her.

His slow, steady snoring sang from the cabin's couch. She curled up on the bed, smiling softly at her good fortune.

CHAPTER 33

Fern, nothing if not true to her word, spent the next few days exhausting and exhilarating the limits of Shiloh's brain. The tiny cottage transformed into a nest of sorts, surrounding Shiloh with so much new knowledge about natural psychokinesis that her mind spun. She doubled down on her efforts and took pride in committing a shocking number of details to memory.

Shiloh could tell her obsessive dedication to the lessons worried Fern, but she shrugged off her mentor's encouraging hints to slow down or take a break. She needed to prepare for the meeting tonight. She didn't know what to expect, but her skin prickled in anticipation.

She had kept Mariam's request a secret despite her newfound confidence in Fern. A well-meaning, but unwelcome intervention from her new friend could cost her this chance, and she couldn't take the risk. Emotions swirled as the minutes ticked by, passing both quicker and more slowly than Shiloh would have liked. She fidgeted, tapping her foot against her chair leg, and Fern started growing both suspicious and annoyed. Shiloh compulsively checked the rusted antique wall clock on the far wall. It hung nestled between glass jars and read 6:31 p.m. Thirty-three minutes until dusk.

Shiloh racked her brain and an ounce of panic crept in. *What do I tell Fern? How do I get out of the cottage without arousing any more suspicion than she already has?* She was a horrible liar, especially under pressure.

Sausage-sized fingers snapped two inches from the end of Shiloh's nose and brought her out of her thoughts. She gave a little jump in her chair before focusing on Fern.

"You need a break. I'm putting my foot down and insisting," declared Fern sternly. "You're going googly-eyed from all this research I'm shoving down your throat. You have a new assignment. Take a walk through the woods and try to sense the energy of the natural world around you. Leave all your electronics behind and, yes, that includes your phone. Lose yourself in the woods for a little while."

Shiloh could have leapt up and hugged the bear of a woman. She couldn't have asked for a better opportunity but fought to keep her cool.

"I don't know…" Shiloh feigned uncertainty, hoping her tone sounded convincing.

"This assignment isn't optional." Then after a pause she added, "Okay, don't actually get lost, but take your time. The learning path here in my lab isn't prescriptive, despite your efforts to make it so. You need to clear your head if you want to start practical application of anything I've taught you."

"You're right. I'm so wound up I can barely find my own current let alone sense the subtleties of the world around me," Shiloh replied, letting out an exaggerated sigh of frustration. She stood and pushed her chair back from the table with more gusto than required.

Equal parts satisfaction and surprise registered in Fern's expression, but she didn't press the issue. "Take a coat. It's going to get cold soon. And be careful. None of the animals in the forest will hurt you, but all the same..."

Shiloh allowed Fern to bundle her in a large flannel jacket. It could have fit an entire second person inside, but she had to admit the jacket did leave her warm and cozy. Fern rubbed Shiloh's shoulders affectionately before giving her a nudge out the door.

"Enjoy. See if you can find the current of something small and slow. Maybe a dandelion. I don't expect you'll get it the first go but just try anyway."

Nodding, Shiloh headed off. She circled around the back of the cottage and followed the barely visible dirt trail winding into the forest. To keep up appearances, Shiloh forced herself to meander slowly until she was out of sight from the cottage. She then doubled back and camouflaged herself in the trees, picking her way toward the small clearing her mother had indicated. It was a little close to the house for her liking, but she didn't dare deviate from the plan.

As she walked, she remained conscious of her breathing, coaxing her heart rate back down to normal despite the adrenaline pumping through her. Sweating in the heavy jacket, she found a discreet place to hide and swiftly tucked herself behind a cluster of trees. She faced the house to make sure she would know if Fern came looking for her.

Her nerves bounced around like Mexican jumping beans. She didn't even bother trying to make any kind of meaningful connection with the natural world like Fern had suggested.

Shiloh held her breath as she waited. Before she left, Fern's watchful eye had scrutinized every move, making sure she left all her electronics behind. This included her smart watch, so she couldn't track the minutes until dusk anymore. The hair on her arms stood on end in anticipation. Her heart beat in her throat, threatening to burst at any minute. Her mother, the ghastly, skinny shadow of a woman from the cabin would be here soon.

Shiloh's eyes strained as daylight vanished by the minute. A sudden shudder, ferocious as an electric shock, ran down her spine. The chorus of crickets amplified their chirps, sounding like a blasting stereo to her heightened senses. She cursed them, impatience and anxiety pounding.

Then a sensation she had only experienced once crashed into her. The high, soft at first, quickly intensified, and soon Shiloh was once again floating in that semi-lucid trance from the library.

Mom? she asked tentatively, leaning into the connection.

Shiloh, a soft, buttery voice answered back. *My girl, I've missed you so much. I'm sorry I had to leave you so soon the other night. I'm weak by myself.*

Mom, let me help you, Shiloh pleaded. *I don't know why he took you, but you have to come with me. Where are you? I want to see you.*

I'm here, Mariam responded gently, but no movement accompanied the voice.

Oh, Mom, I missed you. Nothing was right after you left. I knew you weren't dead though; I just knew it. Shiloh's words tumbled out in a torrent of pent-up emotion. *Come on. You remember Fern, right? We can go see her. She can help you. We'll get you a doctor... you didn't look well last time I saw you.*

The faintest outline of an angular, sickly woman appeared on the other side of the clearing.

Shiloh couldn't hold back any longer. She ran, not caring that she was in full view of the cottage and threw her arms around her mother. They both nearly toppled, and Shiloh had to support Mariam's slight frame to keep her from falling over. Shiloh trembled, barely able to contain the happy tears threatening to spill over. She was really here. This had felt impossible for so many years yet here they were.

Mariam held on to her daughter for a brief moment before gently extracting herself from Shiloh's arms.

Shiloh, she said, eyes darkening. *That's not why I'm here. I've told you, but you aren't listening. I don't want to leave Draven. He's my soulmate and intellectual equal. We're working to harness the most powerful forces in the world. But we need you. Only then can we actuate our plan to control free will and save the world from itself.*

Shiloh froze.

No, Mom. You aren't well. What are you talking about— controlling free will? You aren't making sense. Your mind isn't clear, but let me help you. You can come back to the university. We can work together there. Amazing research is happening, and your old friends would be over the moon to have you back. Draven is… bad, Mom. He almost killed Margaret.

Mariam shook her head. *No, no. He didn't mean that. You just don't understand him like I do. Margaret just got in the way. He was trying to make you understand what you're missing. Shiloh, please. I love you. I want to share my life's work with you, but you must come with me. We live in the glass house. It's marvelous, my darling.*

Mariam's eyes looked glassy, pleading, but somehow still vacant. It chilled Shiloh to the core.

But, Mom, come with you where? Where is the glass house? Shiloh prodded, remembering her original mission.

I can't tell you, but I can show you. Why are you asking so many stupid questions, Shiloh? Don't you even care about me? Our energy, our connection, is special. You're my daughter and that is the most powerful bond on Earth. Maybe if you won't listen to me, you'll listen to him, Mariam admonished in agitation.

She grabbed Shiloh's wrist hard, and Shiloh yelped as much from surprise as pain. Mariam whirled around and tugged Shiloh deeper into the forest. As they wove expertly between trees, the path opened up and… there he stood. Ghastly pale with hair black as midnight, Draven stood with open arms, as if waiting for a hug.

Mariam let go of Shiloh and folded into his arms, kissing him deeply on the mouth.

This was all wrong. Shiloh stopped, paralyzed and unsure how to react. Although she hadn't believed her mother capable of hurting her, she knew Draven had no problem causing pain.

Now, they stood face-to-face.

Let her go, Shiloh communicated, aiming her focus at Draven. Even to her, the words sounded meek.

Who? Mariam? She's free to go whenever she likes. She doesn't want to leave. We're a team. A dyad. But we need our third to make a triad, he explained, his tone patronizing.

I don't want anything to do with you. I want my mother, and I want to go home. You've stolen so much. I won't let you keep taking, Shiloh communicated fiercely. She hoped the shaking that surely would have been present in her audible voice would not come through in her brain-to-brain communication.

She shook her head, trying and failing to clear it. The floating feeling distracted her. It made her mind fuzzy and her thoughts blurry around the edges. She was prepared this time, though. She steeled herself, willing the logical part of her consciousness to maintain control over the emotional part.

Shiloh, I don't think you understand how important our work is. We're going to control the variables, Draven reminded her, repeating the familiar refrain. *Imagine if you had the power to make sure you and those you love couldn't get hurt anymore. If you could prevent undesirable events, like horrible car accidents?* He winked.

A cold bead of sweat trickled down her spine. Her thoughts raced and she hoped he couldn't sense her terror.

Just think, Shiloh. We could pull the strings to make world peace possible, Mariam added.

How? How could you possibly do that? Listen to yourself, Shiloh snapped back.

If we can connect to people, both ordinary and extraordinary, the same way the three of us are connected to each other and to the forest right now, we can influence them. Make sure they can't make a terrible mistake, Draven cut in.

And, you never have to feel sad again, Shiloh. This current from the trees is magical. Don't you feel this ecstasy and energy? It cured my deepest depression. Because of this miracle I've been able to pave this path to greatness. Mariam spun in a circle, gesturing as she spoke.

Ignoring this statement, Shiloh tried to sneer at Draven.

Draven either didn't notice or didn't care, but her mother did. Mariam walked over and slapped Shiloh hard across the face, causing her to stumble and trip on a nearby tree root. She fell hard to her hands and knees. Masculine laughter emanated from Draven, his voice thundering through the trees. Mariam returned to his side, but he turned and smacked her hard, mirroring her assault on Shiloh.

Before Shiloh could react to either blow, Draven strode up behind her and pushed her head into the earth. Maniacal cackling trickled from his mouth. Face down in the dirt and panic setting in, Shiloh bucked her hips up, but he sat on her as if riding a horse. A pressure and then a sting on the back of her neck registered. Her body froze as he whispered aloud in her ear, "We *will* do this my way. You *will* play by my rules and my rules alone."

He roughly released her. Slowly, Shiloh pushed herself up, hand rubbing her neck. Something felt wrong back there. She turned over, now facing away from the Earth and stared into his steel eyes. The pieces of the puzzle starting to fall into place. "You've drugged her. She's an addict. Are you happy playing God?"

"Playing God? What a foolish thing to say. We all know God is a social construct. Science alone makes this world what it is. I'm combining the most gifted humans with the most powerful untapped energy on the planet." He made a point to pause and look between Mariam and Shiloh. "I'm achieving greatness, and with that responsibility comes the identification and control of every variable."

Stunned, Shiloh stared at Draven and then at Mariam cowering next to him. Her skeletal frame shivered violently, the warmth of the sun now gone.

How could this haggard, beaten, weak victim be my mother?

The smart, strong, kind woman Shiloh remembered had thoroughly explained the logistics of why monsters could not hide under beds and the science behind why eating vegetables would make you grow taller. Mariam had been her idol. Seeing her mother reduced to broken pieces this way cracked something deep inside Shiloh.

In the distance, twigs crackled, and the sound of heavy footsteps sliced through the thick air between them. Shiloh recognized the sound of Fern's heavy stride.

Mariam jumped like a startled doe. Draven looked sharply at Shiloh.

Who did you tell about this meeting? he asked, switching back to brain-to-brain communication.

Nobody, Shiloh cried, unsure if she wanted to keep Draven and Mariam here or push them far, far away.

We have to go. We can't get caught here, Draven said, alarm registering in his voice. *Shiloh, come with us. You must come. That's the only way you get to keep your mother.*

I won't be a part of your sick plan. You can't just control the bad out of the world. That's ludicrous. Shiloh's heart broke as she communicated the words. She knew she couldn't go, but the thought of her mother slipping away once again...

So caught up in social constructs yet again. Who gets to define right and wrong? Your fake God? Wrong is powerful leaders dictating the lives of millions under the guise of political agendas. War is wrong. Pain is wrong. But influencing the odds into your favor? That isn't wrong. That's opportunity. You'll regret this. This is your last chance. I'm not going to play nice anymore, Draven warned.

Shiloh stood and gulped, feeling the full weight of the choice before her. She swiveled, straining to check Fern's distance. If she just had another minute to think, she could figure this out. She would know the right answer. She couldn't bear the thought of losing her mother, but she also couldn't give in to Draven's perverse ideology.

"Shiloh!" Fern's thunderous voice bellowed her name through the trees. When she turned back to face Draven and Mariam, she found the clearing in front of her empty.

Her connection to Draven and Mariam and the forest splintered, and she fell from the highest of highs to the depths of despair in one fell swoop.

This must be what detox feels like.

Numb, Shiloh's feet remained planted to the forest floor. She must have looked as awful as she felt because when Fern saw her, she rushed over and engulfed Shiloh in her arms, swallowing the whole of her form into a comforting embrace.

"She's gone. She's not herself anymore. My mom... she isn't coming back."

CHAPTER 34

He held the gun to the back of her head. Her breath rose and fell in time with the howling wind as she slept. Tree branches, camouflaged by the night, relentlessly battered the roof.

His hand, almost subconsciously, rubbed the scar on the back of his neck.

He angled the barrel up, finding the bottom of her skull and then moving to the top of her C1 vertebra.

Slowly. Carefully. Slightly to the left. There.

Click.

No reaction. Not a single hitch in her breathing, her nightmare clearly undisturbed.

He wiped a pinprick of blood from the back of her neck, the tiny wound in her flawless skin already starting to scab.

Just as he had hoped. He had given her the greatest gift.

CHAPTER 35

They stood out in those dark, comforting woods for a long, long time. Wind gently ruffled the leaves, giving the illusion of a calm fall evening, but Shiloh and Fern now knew what those limbs concealed. The sharp betrayal of the tree branches bore through like an axe. Evil lurked in every shadow. Fern held Shiloh close like a child, and Shiloh allowed herself to get lost in her dark thoughts.

Finally, Fern took Shiloh's hand and led her back to the cottage. Shiloh's senses, dampened and muted after the incredible high of her connection with the forest, made her paranoia almost unbearable. She kept turning around, sensing a presence, but nothing ever materialized. The tiny hairs on the back of her neck stood on end.

At the cottage, Fern built a fire in the ancient wood-burning fireplace and poured piping hot tea into ceramic mugs.

Shiloh was beyond tears, her heart nothing more than a dreidel, trying to stay upright while her mind spun and threatened to throw her off kilter. Fern didn't push her to speak but instead waited patiently.

After a few sips of tea and a deep, calming breath, Shiloh started at the beginning. Facing Fern on the overstuffed sofa, she rehashed the entire week, starting with the night in the library. Her voice shook with fear, but Fern, to her credit, didn't interrupt even once.

Despite her lack of words, Fern's face read like an open book. Shiloh could see her new mentor join the emotional roller coaster she had been riding alone until now. She also registered the hurt in Fern's eyes at being lied to.

A long silence stretched when she finished what felt like an epic tale. Rubbing the back of her sore neck, Shiloh waited, expecting a waterfall of questions. Instead, Fern studied Shiloh, as if she were a scientific anomaly.

"Why didn't you tell me?" Fern finally asked, her voice low and trembling with emotion.

The guilt Shiloh had been fighting back flooded her, drowning out all her other feelings. She had always been such a people-pleaser and she hated this about herself. She dreaded the inevitable disappointment and anger of others after making a mistake. Particularly when it came from someone as kind and patient as Fern. Particularly when she deserved it.

"I'm sorry..." she whispered, grappling for the right words. "I thought if I told you, you wouldn't have let me go and I'd miss out on her forever. I know you want to help... I just thought... I thought I could handle it if I learned everything you taught me."

Fern nodded the way she always did while considering an alternative point of view. Unlike other mentors Shiloh had encountered throughout her life, Fern did genuinely try to walk in the shoes of others, no matter where they came from.

"As much as I'd like to disagree, and as much as I disapprove of your tactics, you're right. I wouldn't have let you go, not alone and maybe not at all," Fern agreed.

Shiloh rolled her eyes.

"That's because I care about you," she added gently. "That risk you took… it was stupid at best, reckless at worst. Why can't you see that? You're so incredibly bright, yet sometimes… so selfish. You could've gotten yourself killed, helped absolutely nobody, and left a world of hurt behind you. We can't lose you like we lost Mariam."

This response landed like a punch in the gut. Shiloh hadn't considered that her well-being would have any effect at all on Fern and the others. In fact, she had assumed they would be relieved if she could solve this on her own. Instead of responding, she looked down at her shoes and psychokinetically played with their laces.

"What do you make of it?" Fern finally asked.

"Of what?" Shiloh responded, almost automatically.

"All of it. What do you make of it?"

"Well…" Shiloh paused, unsure how to continue. "How much did you see? I mean out in the woods?"

"Enough to see she's different," replied Fern, wistfully.

Shiloh looked at Fern with eyes begging for further explanation that would make it all come together.

She wasn't always this way, Fern said, switching to brain-to-brain.

This tiny gesture of intimacy almost made Shiloh smile. Though she and Margaret nearly always communicated without audible words, Fern had never extended her this privilege.

What was she like? I mean as you remember her? Shiloh asked.

Fern switched back to normal speech. "She was… inquisitive, but in the best way possible. Full of life. I remember once she had stayed at the lab late, unable to pry herself away from her textbooks. She completely lost track of time. When

I discovered her on my way out, I convinced her to walk with me and get some air. As usual, her mind bounded a million miles ahead of the science, and her enthusiasm was contagious. We sat down on the grass in the middle of campus and watched the sun set…" Fern trailed off, smiling at the memory.

Shiloh could picture it. She had sat on that same grass with Simon and Wendel, studying for exams.

Fern got up and opened a desk drawer, rummaging as she continued to tell the story. "We were getting absolutely eaten alive by mosquitos, but it was such a perfect night we couldn't bring ourselves to go inside. All of a sudden it started pouring. The clouds came out of nowhere, and before we could even gather our things, we were completely soaked. Then the lightning started, and it was breathtaking. Instead of rushing for cover like I had started to do, Mariam covered her bookbag with her jacket and then spread her arms wide, turned her face to the sky, and began to cry."

"I had no idea what the problem was until she said to me, 'How can energy be this amazing? It's mind-blowing. That lightning, I've never seen anything like it. It inspires me in a way I've never felt before.'"

Fern had started making her way back to Shiloh with a small slip of paper in her hand.

"At that time, I was caught up in myself and my work, and it had been ages since I stopped to appreciate the wonders of the world. Mariam helped me completely reframe my world and honestly inspired the work I do today. The miracle of nature's energy," Fern declared. Then she handed Shiloh a small Polaroid picture. "We took this at her PhD graduation ceremony."

An excited Fern and a beautiful, fuller version of Mariam beamed out of the frame, both looking positively radiant. Looking at the picture vivified Shiloh's hazy childhood memories of her mother. The beautiful, thick hair and fair complexion created a striking contrast. For the first time, Shiloh realized how much she looked like her mother at this age. Fern looked exactly the same despite the many years that had passed.

"Keep it," she urged. Then she circled back to the evening's events. "You know…" She paused. "People change. It's tough to stomach, but it's true."

Shiloh looked up sharply from the image.

"She's damaged, misguided, and maybe even lost forever. I don't know. I can't explain her actions. I'm certain, though, that the Mariam I knew would never, ever hit you."

Shiloh bit her lip, struggling to keep her composure. "The connection with them… it's so strong," she stuttered. She wanted Fern to understand the power of that *feeling* but adequate words failed her.

Fern nodded. "That's not unheard of. I mean it is, but we understand it."

"We do?" Shiloh asked, not understanding at all.

"Well, the flooding of your neural pathways causes your brain to activate your mesolimbic dopamine system but interferes with the communication system and causes dopamine to build up. I assume you feel sluggish?"

"Very…" Shiloh replied, shaking her head in an attempt to clear the mental block clouding her brain.

"That's to be expected. Breaking a connection of that magnitude is nearly identical to coming down from a drug high. You should get some rest, but before you do, I want to confess something to you…"

Shiloh's ears perked and she clenched her jaw, dreading Fern's revelation.

"I haven't been totally honest either," Fern whispered, as if speaking in confidence. Then her words tumbled out so rapidly Shiloh could barely follow. "I mean, I've told you a half truth, like what you did to me. No hard feelings, though. At least not on my end."

"Me either," Shiloh muttered, still ashamed.

"Anyway, I told you about my theory that death is a force, and one goal of my work is indeed to prove it. However, I didn't tell you why…" She paused appraising Shiloh and wringing her hands nervously.

"The currents in all living things are connected. This is a common belief, but nobody's been able to prove it, let alone harness it in any meaningful way. I believe death is the biggest disruptor to the fabric of that connectivity. When life and death collide and exist simultaneously, just for a nanosecond, both their energies are combined, forming the most powerful electromagnetic connection on Earth."

Shiloh studied Fern, trying to gauge how to respond. Indices of physics, biology, and psychomanipulation facts spun in her mind like an old-fashioned rolodex. In that moment, the roles felt reversed. Shiloh played the teacher and Fern the student, steeling herself for the onslaught of criticism about to follow.

Finally, Shiloh decided to steal Fern's line from a few days ago. "Tell me your theory."

Just as Shiloh had done, Fern whizzed into explanation mode. Shiloh had to stop her a few times to make sure she followed. She prided herself in being a good student but Fern's work, complex and enormous, took everything she thought she knew to a whole new level. The equations flowed together like a practiced speech, both complex and eloquent, and by the time Fern finished, Shiloh could hardly believe it. The idea blared like a horn, so obvious. It both frustrated and amazed Shiloh that this basic, connective energy that flowed literally everywhere life and death existed could be so difficult to capture.

That part stumped Fern every time. The timing eluded her. She couldn't seem to harness that singular, fleeting moment; the lag in all the devices she tried, including her most recent "Current Counter," too big an obstacle to surmount. Despite trying for years, nothing worked.

Fern's agitation grew as she continued to share, and Shiloh saw a glimpse of the passionate, fiery researcher inside. The dark of night enveloped the cottage, but neither Shiloh nor Fern noticed as they ideated.

"I think we need to look at this through a new lens," Shiloh suggested. She pulled Draven's twisted manifesto from the back cover of her planner and set it flat on the table between them.

Banish the cruelty of the past.
But let its pain fuel the power of the future.

Light invites attention, visibility, and torment.
Dark yields invisibility, and invisibility yields invincibility.

Only those trusting of darkness understand how connection percolates under its protection.
Only those who embrace darkness harbor any hope of realizing their true power.

Together, Mariam and I will achieve ultimate control of the human consciousness.
We will own the darkness together.
Become the greatest force of all time.
And eliminate the pain people cause each other.

Far too many remain unworthy of the privilege of psycho-manipulation.
Just because a bud grows on a rose bush, that doesn't mean a flower must bloom.
Mariam knows this.
She is my perfection, my equal in every way.

Her light conjoined into my dark.
We will be the gatekeepers of the mind.
With the forest as our salvation, power, and lifeforce.
Stronger than death, we will reign.

This is the foreboding.

"Sounds like the ravings of a lunatic to me," Fern spouted, her voice dripping in sarcasm.

"Well, Draven's definitely a lunatic, but he's a powerful one. At the end he talks about lifeforce and death. We know he can connect to the forest, so he has to have figured out how to at least make that large-scale connection," Shiloh reasoned.

"What does he know that we don't?" Fern mused. "He talks about reigning stronger than death… Damnit what am I missing?" She pounded the palm of her hand on the table, rattling the glass bottles lining the shelved walls.

"Do you think he's figured out how to harness the lifeforce connectivity? Maybe use it to overpower death? Darkness might not be literal darkness. He could be using it as a euphemism here. Is that what he means by 'own the darkness'?"

"Maybe," Fern replied, head in her hands. "I don't know though… it just seems like a reach. No offense, but why not just kill you when you refused to go with him and be done with the whole mess?"

"I think he needs my mind for his plan. My mom said something about our connection being super powerful because we are daughter and mother…"

They both slumped, and Shiloh, unable to fight the hangover-like symptoms pounding through her body any longer, soon dozed off in the reading nook under Fern's window.

* * *

Smack. A furry missile hit Shiloh right in the face, rudely startling her awake. A slipper. The gentle breeze from the night before had blossomed into a fierce, howling wind battering at the window to which her cheek was stuck. *How could it be morning already?* She didn't even remember falling asleep.

Rubbing the crust from her eyes, Shiloh observed a bustling Fern packing up what appeared to be a picnic for ten and a bag big enough for an extended holiday. Puzzled, Shiloh opened her mouth to inquire when Fern threw some more clothes at her.

"Hurry, get dressed! We have to go. Margaret's coming home!"

Shiloh could hardly believe her ears and needed no further prompting. She threw on the mismatched clothes and raced out the door. Fern strode ahead and Shiloh struggled to keep up while carrying the giant picnic basket. No amount of persuasion could convince Fern to leave any bit of it at home. Margaret would be hungry, after all.

Fern's company made the bumpy bus ride much more pleasant, and Shiloh settled in as comfortably as she could. While they drove, she pulled her planner out of her bag and began to write. It had been through so much with her and the ritual comforted her racing mind. Unlike her usual notes, these scrawls didn't capture to-dos but rather observations about her mother.

Wrapped up in her task, Shiloh didn't realize they'd arrived at the hospital until Fern tugged impatiently at her hand and herded her off the bus. As they walked in, Shiloh tore the page out of her planner and threw it in the trash.

My stupid list won't bring her back, so what does it matter?

The nurse who met them in the waiting room insisted they be quiet and gentle with Margaret, but as soon as they saw her upright and awake, Fern and Shiloh both started shouting their greetings.

"Margaret, my dear. Oh, you had me so worried. I've missed you!" Fern raced to the bedside, and Shiloh nearly tripped over the abandoned bag in the middle of the room.

Shiloh decided separating the two women would be impossible, so instead she inserted herself into the greeting by wrapping her thin arms around Margaret from the back and resting her head on the older woman's back.

"I missed you. I missed you. I missed you! Don't ever scare me like that again!" Shiloh cried. Then she quickly added, "Thank you." She might have let a few tears of joy spill over but quickly wiped them away before Margaret could see.

The nurse eventually gave up on formalities and left the three alone, shutting the door on the chaotic, too-loud reunion.

"Shiloh, my girl. Have you been practicing, I hope? We cannot get Mariam back unless you are at the top of your game," Margaret stated, turning to meet Shiloh's eye.

Shiloh's stomach flip-flopped, realizing she was going to have to tell Margaret about the degenerated state of her mother. "Yes, ma'am. I've come a long way, thanks to Fern."

Fern smiled fondly, and an immense sense of gratitude blossomed in Shiloh's chest.

They hired a taxi back to the university. Fern insisted Margaret stay at the cottage while getting back on her feet. Shiloh would have bet money against Margaret accepting any help from anyone, but her relationship with Fern seemed different, sisterly in a way. Shiloh and Fern both stared at Margaret the whole ride home, watching anxiously for any signs of discomfort or distress.

At the cottage, Fern settled Margaret onto the couch, tucking her in so tightly that the many blankets and pillows nearly swallowed her tiny frame. Fern went through the events of the past few weeks with remarkable care, and Margaret eagerly asked the questions she hadn't been able to when she was in the hospital.

For once, Fern did most of the talking and Shiloh gratefully reverted to the comfort of introversion. She added details here and there, but unsurprisingly, Fern gave thorough and considerate explanations, particularly when they had to do with Mariam.

Margaret and Shiloh quietly held hands, and Fern stroked Jigsaw's marbled shell. The air in the room hung heavily with what felt like dread to Shiloh, and it seemed nobody knew where to go next. Margaret and Fern had locked eyes, and Shiloh suspected they were connecting directly, but she didn't know how to insert herself into the connection.

Shiloh let out a frustrated huff, and Fern smiled apologetically. "Margaret wanted to know if I'd told you the part about my research into life's connectivity. I assured her we could all speak freely here."

Out of nowhere it seemed, Margaret doubled over and grabbed her head in her hands. She fell to her knees next to the couch as Shiloh watched in horror. Fern and Jigsaw materialized at Margaret's side in the blink of an eye.

"What? What is it? Tell me what's wrong. Talk to me, Marg," Fern encouraged.

Shiloh froze, unable to think of something useful to do. After what felt like minutes, not seconds, Fern lifted Margaret's writhing frame back onto the couch. Margaret contorted as if wrestling with a snake wrapped around her head. Then just as quickly as the fit started, it stopped.

Shiloh had managed to get her phone out to dial 911, but Fern gently pushed it away.

"No need. Marg. Marg! Talk to me. Tell me what happened," Fern prodded.

The shutters of the cottage banged loudly against the house, and one of them even blew shut as if in answer to Fern's question.

Margaret slumped back into the cushions of the giant couch and shook her head. "I see and feel things now. Horrible things. It is like treachery takes over my mind and I am powerless in its wake. I thought they were nightmares, but that was the most intense episode yet, and I was not asleep," she cast her eyes to the floor. "I think he is still in me, like

the most intimate of partners. But his infiltration is not con-
sensual. It is psychological rape."

This description shocked Shiloh, horror reverberating in
her bones. She had never considered such a parallel. "What
did you see?" she asked, bracing for the answer.

"Death," Margaret met Shiloh's gaze and then turned to
Fern. "The forest ablaze as far as I could see. Nothing survived."

CHAPTER 36

He had no one to blame but Mariam. The girl, stubborn and tenacious, irritated his every nerve. What had he expected from Mariam's only daughter, though?

He knew a mother's love coursed deeply. He couldn't deny that biological curse, and boiling frustration ran hot through his blood at the thought.

A competition for Mariam's affections was one he refused to lose.

Mariam saw this final act as one of contrition after abandoning her only child. But he saw it for what it was. Control.

The three of them could be unstoppable. The energy in the lifeblood connection between mother and child formed the most powerful bond on Earth, after all.

CHAPTER 37

Margaret trembled visibly as she leaned into Shiloh, who sat next to her on the couch. Fern had raced to the backyard to harvest some sort of soothing herb from the garden so she could concoct a natural extract for Margaret, leaving them alone.

"Margaret…" Shiloh began but then stopped, unsure how to proceed.

"My girl, I am so sorry about this whole mess."

"You're sorry? I'm the one who should apologize! This is all my fault. If I hadn't been so stubborn… you're like this because of me… My pride. I thought I could face him, but I've just made a royal mess of everything." Shiloh put her head in her hands.

"This was not your fault. I made a choice. I should not have put you in that sleep pod to begin with. You were not ready. I knew that, but I was selfish. I wanted to find her. To find them."

"I've been doing everything I know how to do to get strong enough to fight him and keep you all out of harm's way, but I'm failing, miserably," Shiloh confessed.

"That is because what you need to do you cannot do on your own. Do you not understand that yet? If you really want to keep us out of harm's way you need to know your limits and start playing on this team."

Shiloh's heart swelled with love for her friend's blatant declaration even as her ego bruised. She had missed Margaret's no-nonsense approach to their relationship. It made trusting her feel safe and real.

Fern chose that moment to reappear, setting down a humungous bowl of soup on the coffee table in front of Margaret. Instead of pointing out the ridiculousness of the portion, Margaret smiled at Fern and started to eat, one tiny spoonful at a time.

"It's a special infusion of nutrition and herbs," Fern declared proudly.

After Margaret had regained her faculties and eaten about a quarter of the soup in the bowl, the three rushed to their safe haven—Leonard's office library. His face fell as he took in Margaret's disheveled appearance, and he wasted no time in calling Simon and Wendel.

Despite the dark circumstances, Shiloh felt a homey sense of family among the musty books and the curious characters in her circle as they all settled in. For the first time, she looked at them as teammates, working to leverage each other's strengths. More importantly, she tested out the idea that she might be an important team member. She hadn't ever really been part of a team.

She and Margaret relaxed into the comforting motions of their conversational tea drinking ritual from the old apartment complex, except this time supporters surrounded them. Shiloh tried to emulate Fern's clear and concise exposition as she rehashed the latest events for the group's benefit.

Leonard nearly fell out of his velvet armchair in anxious excitement when she described Draven pinning her to the forest floor.

Before the group could ask any questions though, Margaret collapsed yet again. This fit lasted even longer than the one at Fern's cottage. Leonard's couch cradled her seizing body, but Shiloh felt the same cold terror as she had only hours before. Even with her team by her side, this incident felt no less scary than the first.

Margaret gasped and moaned when her body stopped shaking, her face ghostly pale in the dim light. Despite the seizure's length, Margaret relayed the contents of her vision almost right away. "A knife," she panted, shaking her head. "Pointed at you, Shiloh."

The room collectively sucked in a sharp breath, and Shiloh's stomach dropped. Leonard repeatedly slicked back his already sweaty hair, stress emanating from his clenched jaw.

"Someone had your wrists bound and was forcing you deep into the forest. Toward the Continental Divide. I could tell the direction from the mountain profiles on the horizon." Gulping, Margaret lay back, as if relaying this information had taken all of her remaining strength.

Gazes throughout the room ping ponged, nobody quite sure how to react. Shiloh's emotional exhaustion started taking its toll, and she didn't know where to start.

How would a team captain respond to such news? She had no idea.

Fern spoke first. "Shiloh, he wants you. He told you as much in the woods. Right?"

Shiloh's hands covered her face, the heels of her hands pressed into her closed eyelids. "Well, not exactly, but based on what my mom said about the power of our bond, I think it's a safe bet. I don't know his endgame, though. He's obsessed with 'controlling the variables,' but I don't know what that means."

She wasn't used to puzzles she couldn't solve, especially scientific ones. Frustrated, she kicked the pillow at her feet across the room like a soccer ball, narrowly missing Wendel's head but causing a few books to fall from the shelf on the far wall. Then she caught herself.

Think like a team.

She collected her emotions before looking to each of her friends. "Whatever it is, he isn't going to leave me alone. And you, Margaret…" she choked a little. "However he did it, he has a direct connection to your brain now. Right?"

Fern and Margaret looked at each other and then, sighing, nodded nearly in unison.

"I do not know how, but that is the most likely explanation," Margaret replied.

"We have to confront him. It's the only way. Go on the offensive. Fern, we need to apply your theory. If he thinks he can be more powerful than death, we need to use the combination of life *and* death to our advantage." Shiloh's head throbbed, a knot forming in the back of her neck.

Margaret, still looking a bit shaky, beamed proudly at Shiloh, focused determination painted on her expression.

Leonard must have been a stage director in his previous life because he sprang into action, sending Simon and Wendel scurrying to bookshelves for resources.

Shiloh took over Leonard's giant chalkboard. "Okay, Fern, where do we start?"

Fern preened. "Well, we need a device that can actually capture the moment between life and death."

"True," Leonard piped in. "But that isn't the beginning. We need our problem statement to start. And our goals."

"Well, the problem is that Draven is super powerful and coming after Shiloh and Margaret," offered Wendel.

"And our first goal should be to stop him!" added Simon.

"True again, lads. But what are the steps to stopping him? I believe first and foremost we need to break his connection with Margaret," said Leonard.

"Then figure out how he's able to maintain control over such massive energy stores," said Fern. "And then stop him from wielding them against us."

Shiloh smiled at Fern's use of the word us. She made a list as they spoke, falling naturally into her role of organizing the chaos.

"Then we need to eliminate him." Margaret's eyes clouded, and they looked a shade darker than usual. She focused her attention on Leonard, ignoring the others.

The group fell silent. Heaviness cloaked the initial excitement of the planning.

"Right-o then," Leonard clapped his hands. "No time like the present to get started."

They poured themselves into research taking full advantage of both Leonard's private library and the university resources.

Then Fern had an idea. "HAARP! It's a research station in Alaska! I've heard rumors of significant activity up there exploring utilization of high frequency transmitters to control natural forces like the weather."

"Maybe that's how he does it!" Leonard interrupted, throwing his current pile of scratch paper in the air, creating a dramatic confetti of scribbles. "Maybe he has a device he can leverage to tap into the trees, or at least a specific kind of tree. He seems to have a keen interest in them and thinks they belong to him."

"It's top secret, but desperate times call for extreme measures…" continued Fern. "Can you do it?" She looked over to Wendel and Simon.

"I don't think that's how the saying goes, Fern… But, yes, of course we can." Simon grinned.

It turned out, the pair possessed a suspicious level of technical prowess. They wasted no time hacking into the confidential government research databases. Shiloh was too impressed to be concerned about all the laws they were likely breaking.

These guys really know their stuff.

Fern turned to Leonard. "If Draven's using this technology to maintain control, maybe that control is transferrable. It could be applied to more than just trees… Simon, do we have specs on the HAARP transmission devices in the files?"

"Hold please," he responded, his fingers whizzing.

Fern and Leonard continued their excited banter about the merits of the HAARP research, but Shiloh tuned it out, feeling inexplicably drawn to the bookshelf. Unable to pinpoint the origin of the instinct but trusting it all the same, she allowed her legs to guide her to the ecology section of Leonard's collection.

Her hands moved deftly across the spines of each book and gently felt each of their energy levels until a zing of electricity coursed up her arm. She pulled out a book with yellowed pages and bent corners. The book lay naked without a jacket cover, but when she opened it the title page read *A Natural History of the Forest.*

She flipped through, stopping at a section about a grove of aspens called Pando. Despite being made up of many trees,

Pando was considered one organism. Underground, roots married other roots of the same species and physically linked the individual trees together, creating a vast, interconnected network. Further, each root tip housed a tiny "brain" that allowed each tree to feel pain, breathe, and transmit signals.

Transfixed, she continued to read and reread the section, sensing a significant breakthrough just beyond her grasp. She closed her eyes and visualized the forests from her dreams and from her interactions with Mariam and Draven. As she read further an idea crystallized, and her breath caught.

Connecting directly to the forest was as simple as connecting to a single organism. You didn't need hundreds or thousands of singular connections, just a single entry point to spur a chain reaction. Draven couldn't hold the massive amounts of energy needed for ultra-powerful psychomanipulation, but the collective forest could. By inserting himself as a link at the end of the chain, Draven reaped the benefits of a large-scale connection without bearing the burden of control within his own body. Since the trees were relatively stationary and they naturally connected and communicated with each other, a stable chain reaction might actually be feasible.

Shiloh closed the book and raced to rejoin the group. She gestured wildly and spoke entirely too fast, trying to tell them everything all at once. When she finished, the office stayed eerily silent while everyone processed this new discovery.

"So you're telling me Draven's power comes from a single point of connection that then opens the floodgates for the entire electromagnetic current of the forest to be manipulated at his whim? I can't even imagine the magnitude of that circuit. No wonder he can reach almost anyone, near or far, via direct brain-to-brain connection," mused Fern.

"Biologically, that level of current… No wonder Mariam's addicted!" squeaked Leonard, stopping short.

"If we can make a connection of similar magnitude, or even tap into that existing connection, we stand a chance," Shiloh continued.

"Yes, brilliant, my girl!" cried Margaret. She grabbed Shiloh's chalk, speaking aloud as she added another goal to the list. "Make a more powerful electromagnetic connection than Draven. Or steal his…" She paused. "Not as eloquent as I would have liked, but it will have to do."

Shiloh snatched the chalk back. "How?"

Nobody had noticed Leonard slip out of the room, so when the heavy door slammed, they jumped. "I think I've got just the ticket! The forest is powerful by magnitude of scale. Right? We can do the same thing, but we'll use water. We can connect to the current in the water. If we're lucky, we'll reap the benefits of compounding with the aquatic plant life as well."

At this juncture, Fern took over and thumped Shiloh on the back, just a little too hard. "Shiloh, you were really onto something with your chain reaction theory before. You just had the wrong application!"

"Yeah, pretty smart for a newbie." Simon grinned as he teased.

"Like Fern said, right idea, wrong direction," Wendel chimed in.

"Leonard, you pursue the water angle. I'm going to try and figure out how to tap into the forest network. That seems easier than reinventing the buggy. If Draven can do it, I can do it." Fern set her mouth in a determined line.

The chalk changed hands several times, and the board quickly filled with scrawled ideas, notes, and equations.

Shiloh's organized system had gone to the wind, but she let it go. Her team was committed, and they were really doing this.

The night's flurry of activity paused only briefly to order sandwiches Leonard called "Fat Chickens" from the local campus take-out joint. The subs turned out to be giant Italian rolls bursting with chicken tenders smothered in cheese and gooey sauce. Apparently, the recipe spanned decades, and everyone had experienced their magic except Shiloh.

"These sandwiches absolutely, no doubt, make you smarter," Simon explained through a mouthful of cheese and bread. "It's simply a Revned staple."

Nods of assent swept through the room, and after just one bite, Shiloh understood. The sub warmed her from the inside out, and the huge portion felt exactly right.

The merriment came to a violent halt when Margaret crashed to the floor seizing yet again.

They put pillows beneath her head, but the seizure lasted an unnaturally long time. Despair and helplessness pulsed through the cozy office, Fat Chickens forgotten.

Finally, Margaret stilled. This time, it took her several moments to reorient herself to reality and several more before she could speak coherently. Shiloh breathed out a shaky sigh of relief but couldn't let go of the knot in her stomach. She and Fern sat like bookends on either side of Margaret, huddling close as if their presence could shield their friend from further harm.

"We need to find them. Find him. And fast. He will take your mind, Shiloh. Just like he has taken Mariam's, and he is coming for you soon. Very soon," Margaret finally managed to articulate before slumping down against Shiloh's shoulder, her eyes closed. For the first time in Shiloh's experience, her mentor looked utterly defeated.

Despite Shiloh's lengthy protest, Fern had finally forced her to retire to her rubber apartment after fourteen hours of working in Leonard's library. They were all beginning to get at each other's goats, and Margaret needed to sleep peacefully.

Shiloh conceded the break had likely been much needed when she woke up the next morning and saw the clock read 10 a.m. She never slept that late and had to admit she did feel refreshed.

She sent a quick text to Leonard and jumped in the shower, enjoying the luxury of hot water. Usually he answered messages nearly instantaneously, but when she got out, he still hadn't responded. A tentacle of dread crept into her stomach.

That's not like him.

The weather outside, overcast and gray, personified Shiloh's unease. She grabbed her things and rushed out the door, taking a shortcut through the university center. Despite her anxiety, a little jolt of pleasure coursed through her at the sight of so many fellow students lounging with their books and coffee. She missed that.

She dialed Margaret to check in and offer to bring her tea. Two, three, four rings, but no answer there either. The thread of dread sprouted into fear. Although she hated and often cursed her cell phone, Margaret always picked up for Shiloh.

Forgetting about the drink she ordered at the coffee cart, Shiloh broke into a jog toward the office. Her gut screamed at her that something was very, very wrong.

Leonard's office, dark and moody, looked spooky without any of the usual comfy lighting. She ran cautious fingers across the wood paneling, searching for the light switch. She hit a bump and fumbled before the room illuminated in a familiar yellow glow.

Shiloh screamed, knees going weak. Before her, Leonard slumped unnaturally over the arm of the couch, his eyes open but vacant. Blood trickled down his temple, spattering the off-white collar of his shirt.

"Leonard!" she shook his arm roughly, refusing to believe the worst. A gust of wind from the open window tousled his hair, but he still didn't stir. Frantically, she tapped his cheeks. Squeezed his hand. Knelt next to his face to find his breath. Nothing.

She finally placed two fingers on his neck and waited to feel the throbbing of a beating pulse. Still nothing.

Unwilling to rip her eyes away from the gruesomeness, but also unable to tolerate her proximity to the corpse any longer, Shiloh scuttled backward like a crab. After only a few feet, her left hand squashed a piece of paper, now crumpled from her rapid movement.

Falling to her seat, she turned it over and saw a familiar message.

What the hell is going on?

Draven's manifesto. Word for word. Almost. This time, the last line was crossed out and instead of reading, "This is the foreboding," it read, "The foreboding has arrived."

Not comprehending, Shiloh read and reread that last line. Margaret's handwriting jumped off the page.

CHAPTER 38

The cocky little twit hadn't even seen it coming. Those stupid academics thought they were so smart.

Time to draw the rabbit from the hole. They made it too easy. Such fools. He paced, circling his beautiful house that held his Mariam. Their dreams were so close to realization.

He never could have stayed at Revned, even if they had welcomed him. The politics alone would have mutilated his potential. If that hadn't killed him, the suffocation from their antics and the insufferable obligations that came with the community would have.

This was much, much better.

Manic laughter rumbled from his mouth, and his head lolled back with a great roar.

CHAPTER 39

The forest's ominous canopy blanketed Shiloh's deflated form as she walked, buffering her from the horror of the grisly murder. It dampened her emotions but couldn't fully shield her from the terror. The thick, metallic smell of blood stuck fresh in her throat. Nature's serenity clashed in violent dissonance with her internal chaos.

The events of the morning looped through her mind.

Fern's hulking form blowing through the door. Recognizing Leonard's death. Shaking Shiloh, demanding answers.

"What happened?" she had asked, stern but pleading.

Shiloh could only shake her head, incredulous and helpless. She had fixated her eyes on the heart-shaped mole on Fern's neck and slipped into a trance, unable to meet Fern's gaze.

"Where's Margaret? Have you seen Margaret? Oh goodness, this can't be happening," Fern had cried out, running a hand through her thick, curly hair.

"She wasn't here. Just him," Shiloh gulped, finally finding her voice. She shoved the note deep into her jacket pocket.

"You don't understand. Margaret stayed here last night. We didn't want to move her off the couch after that last seizure. Leonard offered to stay with her."

Shiloh remained silent, unwilling and unable to present Margaret's note. This nightmare kept getting worse. There had to be an explanation.

"Whoever did this must have taken her," Fern continued, looking down at Shiloh. "This is bad. So bad."

Wendel and Simon burst through the heavy wooden door at that moment. Upon registering the scene ahead, their eyes widened in disbelief.

"What the…" Simon started before turning to vomit in the nearby trashcan. Wendel burst into racking sobs.

Their visceral reactions pierced Shiloh like the blade of a knife, and she couldn't bear it. She stormed out of the office and willed herself forward, headed for the woods behind Fern's house. Fists clenched, her body forbade her from stopping to think. Or rather, stopping to hesitate.

Margaret, her strongest ally and closest confidante, loved her friends, especially Leonard. Shiloh had witnessed their unique competitive but affectionate bond, and even sensed a little flirtation between the two.

She couldn't have done this. She couldn't have done this.

Shiloh chanted this mantra in her head, matching the tempo of her heavy footsteps. She didn't bother trying to orient herself to the direction of her travels. Instead, she let her body make the decisions and trusted it to take her where she needed to go. The looming forest didn't intimidate her. Instead, it energized her. The dewy mist slickened her skin as confidence and determination drove her legs forward.

She trudged ahead, and as the forest's thickness grew, so did her anger.

Her raging pulse throbbed in her ears, numb bewilderment giving way to hot fury. First her mother and now her newfound family.

How dare he come after them this way?

She attempted to calm herself by making direct brain-to-brain connections with the trees, the weeds, and even a few insects as she walked. She knew, if nothing else, this would keep her grounded. Each success both surprised and emboldened her in her mission—find Draven.

After what felt like hours, she came across a clearing and her bottled-up emotions spilled over. She screamed, a loud guttural noise. Her voice ached, but she continued, again and again. Lost. Frustrated. Scared. Full of doubt. Her unraveling reverberated, echoing off the rocky mountain cliffs that looked to be a mile away.

How could Margaret have done this?

Despite hiding the note away from the others, it still existed, whether she liked it or not. Whatever the foreboding entailed, she couldn't sit and wait to be told what to do anymore. She refused to continue playing it safe, observing from a distance. She needed to deal with this, and she needed to do it her way.

In that moment she knew, without a doubt, she'd do whatever it took to stop the carnage. If that meant facing Draven alone, she'd oblige.

They were worth it.

Tentatively, Shiloh slowed her breathing and focused her thoughts. The familiar tingling sensation in her fingers grew, and she opened her mind as widely as she could.

Draven? She called. If he didn't respond to her outward screams, maybe he would respond inwardly.

Mom?

Still nothing.

Margaret?

She continued to shuffle toward the cliffs ahead. It seemed as good a direction as any. Her feet began to drag, not from fatigue, but from a deepening dread that grew with each step. The wind whipped at her from all directions, seeming to propel her forward despite her body's resistance.

Then she heard a faint voice in her mind. She couldn't make out the words, but as she closed the distance to the mountain ahead, it clarified.

Meet me on the cliffs, Shiloh, Margaret's voice flooded her mind, and an image of her mentor flashed. *I've been waiting for you.*

The howling wind pushed even harder at her back, trying to speed up the inevitable. Dark clouds descended swiftly overhead and melted into the sun, tightening the knot in Shiloh's stomach. The trek grew more treacherous. Branches and rocks formed handholds as she began to pull herself up the steep mountain, still surrounded by trees. When the incline started to flatten, she didn't hesitate to venture into the dark woods. Margaret's connection grew clearer with each step. No terrain would stop her now.

Something yanked her hair from behind—a quick, unexpected jerk.

A familiar hand clamped over her mouth. Margaret's voice whispered, *Do not move. Do not scream.*

The point of a knife rested on Shiloh's spine. A surprisingly strong shove from Margaret pushed her toward a pile of rocks. Shiloh grasped for the comfort of her old, familiar connection with Margaret, but that felt like banging her head against a concrete wall.

Margaret, what's going on? Why are you doing this? Please stop. Please just talk to me, Shiloh begged.

No matter how desperately she pleaded, Margaret remained silent, impassive. Shiloh managed a wayward glance over her shoulder and could see tears streaming down her mentor's cheeks. When Margaret caught Shiloh looking, a rough push forced her head back around.

As they approached, Shiloh could see they weren't actually headed for a pile of rocks but rather a cave with a slender opening just big enough to slip through. Without warning, Margaret shoved her into the blackness. Instead of solid ground, she felt the familiar sensation of traveling through the closet to Revned.

Where am I going?

Upon emerging, Shiloh initially thought they'd been transported into another part of the world. The darkness, deep as midnight, wrapped around and stuck to her like Saran Wrap. Trees, so many trees, took up every bit of space and spurred her claustrophobia. The muddy ground squelched, protesting her unfamiliar weight as she stepped tentatively forward.

How can a forest be this dense?

Before she could get her bearings, Draven's voice thundered in her mind. It resounded so loudly she nearly toppled over in surprise.

It's about damn time, he sneered. *Finally decided to play by my rules. Did you?*

Shiloh channeled her anger into a forceful response. *No. I'm playing by my own rules.*

The connection grew stronger with each fumbling step, and she could sense his physical proximity even if her eyes couldn't find him.

You're my puppet, you fool. We've been playing you like a fiddle, he replied. *My plan relies on the energy of your "familial ties." Not to mention my darling Mariam wants us to be a family. Doesn't that sound nice?*

Draven's sizable stature appeared through the trees ahead. His pale skin nearly glowed. Shiloh didn't waste any time. Without scruple, she took hold of the branch closest to him, bent it back, and released it in a forceful blow. He reeled, his feet barely staying under him.

He exploded in anger, and Shiloh's head reverberated with the force of his voice. *How dare you use my forest against me?*

She used his moment of his disbelief to create distance between them and take stock of her environment. The coniferous forest stretched widely, vast in every direction as far as she could see. The sun, no more than a faint glimmer through one sparse section of needles, offered no help as a source of light.

A sudden burning blistered up from her spine into her head, fierce as if her brain had caught fire. She crumpled to the ground and grabbed her neck in agony. Pain this intense couldn't exist, yet she felt it all the same.

Then a voice, Draven's voice, overlaid the throbbing. *You think you're so clever. You're just a puppet. You couldn't have made those natural connections without my help. I own you. I'm about to have the power to harness your mind, just as I do with your mother.*

Shiloh froze, pain dulling enough for her to search the darkness for Draven. This lunatic had power over Mariam's mind. *What if she's still in there after all? What if she isn't gone forever?*

As though reading her mind, Draven replied. *I'm not a lunatic. Haven't you been wondering about your stiff neck?*

Shiloh brought her hand up, touching the tender spot. She had attributed it to tension and hadn't even noticed the soft, mosquito-bite sized bump protruding at the base of her skull.

His eyes glittered, an evil smirk painted across his face. *That's no mosquito bite. That, my girl, is the root tip I implanted. Remember when I pinned you down on the forest floor?*

She did but said nothing, instead trying to pinpoint how he could have put something in her body without her realizing it.

As much as I enjoyed that particular segment for my own personal reasons, my goal was singular. The protective bio casing hasn't completely dissolved yet, but it's begun, I see. The tiny brains of each root will soon assimilate with your nerves and cement your connection to the forest and to me.

Alarmed, Shiloh pushed on the bump and then began to scratch. It opened up, and blood collected on her fingertips, but no implant emerged from the wound.

Draven basked in his glory, gloating as Shiloh's eyes widened. *It won't hurt you. If anything, it'll make you happier. You'll feel the high of our botanic connection anytime you want. Or all the time like Mariam if that's your thing. You just have to be patient, so it has time to fully attach.*

I don't want it. I don't want any of that. I want my mother back and my friends safe. That's all, Shiloh responded vehemently.

Draven waved her deepest desires off with a flippant flick of his wrist. *Ah, you will, though. We'll get there. Let's talk about you. Forget those doddering idiots for now.*

Shiloh's mind had started growing bleary, thick with that familiar druggy feeling. She fought it, determined to maintain control of at least her own body.

Seriously, though, what do you see in them? I didn't pin you as the sentimental type, but you've grown so attached. Maybe that big brain of yours isn't all it's cracked up to be.

She stumbled forward to that tiny patch of light. The trees parted a little, and the break gave space for almost enough light to comfortably see.

You even saw my workbench when you came for your little visit. Even after seeing my lovely botanical experiments, you were too stupid to make the connection, Draven continued with a chuckle.

This had to be a dream. A false memory. Something other than reality.

Alas, I must give credit where credit is due, though. After all, none of this would have been possible without my leading ladies. Come on, don't be shy. He licked his dry, cracked lips and stepped to the side, eying Shiloh mischievously.

A strung-out Mariam emerged from the shadows and took Draven by the hand. She stared up at him adoringly. Then a haggard Margaret, looking queasy, stepped out and stood at his other side.

Cold terror iced through Shiloh's veins. The trees moaned, empathizing with her peril. She wanted to cry, scream, call out, but she couldn't find her voice.

The three conspirators circled like hawks zoning in on a field mouse, catapulting Shiloh's mind into overdrive. The sound of crunching gravel and cracking twigs harmonized into an audible din, breaking the silence of the forest.

Tree roots are truly amazing, a fact you may recall but not fully appreciate. They have minds of their own. Not human brains, but rather a structure totally unique. And we can use it. Together, our power is limitless, Draven continued.

She had to do something. But they were all so much better at this than her. Her confidence wavered and she tried to fight of her own self-doubt. Her own anxiety. Panic wasn't an option.

Shiloh bolted, branches ripping her clothes as she ran. She had run about one hundred yards before a sharp pain through her temples caused her to reel over and slam into the nearest trunk. A rogue branch scraped her cheek, narrowly missing her eye.

She spun in a half circle to try and right herself, but Draven loomed too close. She took off in the opposite direction, knowing she could move faster on foot than the lumbering man and the two broken women at his flanks. The thick foliage created a challenging barrier, though, and her nimbleness began to fail.

Her mind reeled trying to figure out the consequences of the root-tip implant. He said it would soon connect her to him and the forest and Mariam. She had to assume Margaret had been compromised by a similar biodevice.

She had to fight the inevitable as long as possible.

Ducking behind the trunk of a massive evergreen, Shiloh shuddered and, after a deep breath, tried to plunge her fingers into the back of her head. Nothing. A wave of nausea followed by lightheadedness caused her to fall sideways into the tree. How deep did the roots run? Were they already latching on to her own nerves?

Heavy footsteps drew nearer.

This safe haven won't stay safe for long.

To Shiloh's horror, Mariam came at her, jumping on her back and clawing at the hood of her sweatshirt. More stunned than hurt by the tiny woman's attack, Shiloh stumbled. The stench of Mariam's body odor and greasy hair polluted the clean forest air.

Then Draven descended. Shiloh didn't know from which direction. He crushed her and her mother together into what could have been considered a hug under other circumstances and slapped a pair of handcuffs on them, binding their wrists to each other.

Shiloh had stopped struggling, but her muscles remained coiled, ready for action. Mariam turned to Shiloh and kissed her forehead. The unexpected tenderness of the gesture tore at Shiloh's heartstrings.

How many times over the years did I dream of getting just one more kiss goodnight from my mother?

Then Draven's hand at their backs forced them through the branches at a rapid pace. As they walked, Mariam grabbed Shiloh's hand. The familiar euphoria from their previous connections had started to creep its way from Shiloh's mind into her core. She couldn't help but smile. Despite her logical brain's protests, a carefree mood clawed its way inside her. Soon she would be high as a kite.

A glass house, *the* glass house, from her sleep pod connection with Draven, materialized in front of them. She felt herself being shoved inside with her mother in tow.

"You should be comfortable here until I'm ready for you," Draven smirked, speaking aloud for the first time. He slammed the door upon his departure, leaving Shiloh and Mariam alone.

Mariam breathed a sigh of relief. "Thank God we're back," she cooed. "I'm so glad you're here to feel this with me. This happiness. You never have to suffer again. I know I've caused you so much pain, but I'll make it up to you. I promise."

Shiloh couldn't think. She fought the happy bliss threatening to take over and tried to remain calm. Those perfect words spoken from her mother's mouth encompassed everything she wanted to hear, but she knew they weren't real. The sincerity with which Mariam spoke broke Shiloh's heart yet again.

Who knew one heart could be broken into so many pieces? True heartbreak didn't happen once, straight down the middle like the illustrated heart emoticon led you to believe, she reflected. Rather, the people and the memories you held most dear fissioned under the pressure of tiny cracks, built up by blow after blow. Eventually the pressure became too much, and your heart simply crumbled.

This sad, miserable realization gave Shiloh a bizarre, determined strength. She dragged Mariam over to the wall and kicked at the glass. Her effort resulted in a mild thud that reverberated around them, but nothing more. She felt utterly useless, both mentally and physically drained from the overstimulation.

She wasn't going to make it out of here. Her failure hit hard yet again.

Maybe it wasn't worth it. Maybe none of it really mattered after all. Who got to decide right and wrong anyway? She wasn't religious. Maybe, if she stayed, she could find her mother deep down inside. Maybe together they could fight Draven. Maybe they really could be a family. Maybe, maybe, maybe…

The burning sensation in her mind exploded, once again crippling her resolve. This time it lasted even longer than the previous episodes and she fell to the floor. When she emerged from her writhing state, Mariam was stroking her hair.

My love, my love, my girl, my love, she sang. *Little Bo-Peep may have lost her sheep, but I never have to lose you again.*

A happy memory flooded Shiloh's senses. That had been their rhyme.

A small Shiloh lay in her little green bed clutching her favorite stuffed toy. A sheep. She begged her mother to tell the story just one more time. One more time before they had to say goodnight.

You can stay here, or there in the feeling of your most joyful memories, forever my love. That's what I do. He can give you that. Don't you see? Mariam whispered softly, a smile playing at her voice.

Shiloh drifted away, giving in to the dark comfort lulling her to sleep.

CHAPTER 40

Draven craved a challenge, but it kept eluding him.

That silly man had basically offered himself up to for sacrifice. Smitten fool. Had he really thought he could change Margaret's fate? Leonard was clearly too dense for this level of artistry.

Maybe she would give in to him. That silly, stubborn Shiloh. If Mariam hadn't enslaved his heart long ago, he would just dispose of the two of them and start over. But he couldn't even consider it now.

The promise of coming days loomed, almost too much to bear. Anticipation caused him to salivate, his sweaty palms wringing, foot tapping.

Tap. Tap. Tap.

Execution was paramount, rapture imminent. Amplification of control, the ultimate prize. So much at stake.

He would harness his evergreens, and then he would annihilate the shackles holding him back.

CHAPTER 41

Everything made so much sense in this dream. Shiloh and Mariam lay side by side, trying to find the brightest star in the sky. It remained black, though, and instead of stars, shiny raindrops assaulted them, flinging the silent night into a roaring cacophony. Then it wasn't rain anymore, but beads of glass. So much glass. Shards of it showered down from the heavens, pelting every exposed inch of Shiloh's skin. Too small to cut, the impact of the pellets stung like an army of bees.

A hand shook Shiloh's shoulder, violently yanking her upper body from the ground. She blinked, scanning the area to try and orient to her surroundings. She thought she'd been inside a house, but now the cold mountain air bombarded her senses, and everything rushed back all at once.

Glass covered every surface, but instead of a transparent roof overhead, tree branches formed a loose canopy over the remains of the structure. The cabin had fallen.

"Fern?" Shiloh questioned, unable to make sense of the figure before her.

"No time," Fern hissed.

She wasn't dreaming. Mariam lay on the floor next to Shiloh, covered in a layer of glass. She looked like an ice sculpture. Her chest rose and fell, an eerily calm expression fixed on her sleeping face.

"How…" Shiloh started with effort, still feeling mildly drugged.

"I followed you. You didn't think I was going to let you out of my sight. Did you?"

"But I didn't see you," Shiloh tried to begin anew.

"Of course you didn't. I didn't want to you to." Fern pried the handcuffs open, her impossibly large hands apparently also equipped with impossibly strong muscles. "Run! Toward the river. You'll know what to do."

"But…" Shiloh cast a glance at the motionless Mariam.

"Go!" Fern commanded.

She didn't stop to argue. She ran, listening for the faint gurgle of the river she had heard on the way to the cabin. She couldn't overthink this. She had to trust her body.

Every so often she had to pause and listen. After only a couple of minutes, she could smell the river. Then it stretched before her, so near she could touch it. More of a stream up close, but this had to be where Fern meant.

What now?

Shiloh knew better than to think Fern would send her here for no reason. She just had to figure it out.

The grove by the river remained bizarrely quiet except for the crunch of hard earth beneath her feet. The vegetation seemed to lean just slightly back from the water's edge, like it could sense something dangerous.

Bending down to touch the running current, she racked her brain.

Where did our research leave off?

Leonard had wanted to investigate using water the same way Draven used the forest connectivity, but they hadn't made any headway on that front. But that was before… She couldn't think about that now.

How am I supposed to know what to do? She kicked the water's surface in frustration.

Rustling disrupted the silence that had engulfed her, and when she looked back, she startled, spine stiffening. Draven stood barely ten feet behind her. He looked as if he'd been waiting.

"You thought you could shield your thoughts from me? What in the world made you think that? Your implant keeps us connected whether you like it or not," he scolded. "By now, the latching process should be nearly complete."

She couldn't let him get to her. Not now. *If I were Fern, what would I do?*

She looked past Draven and tried, with all her might, to keep the thought at the very periphery of her mind, hopefully out of his grasp.

The plants. Fern had wanted to figure out how to link into Draven's forest connection. Shiloh diverted her attention from the river and started scanning the vegetation.

She saw evergreens, maples, tall prairie grass, and then, the key. Mountain willow. Fern's favorite shrub. She remembered back to the evening last week when her brain had been nearly numb from studying botany textbooks. Fern had taken the books away and brought over one of her specimen bottles. The green leaves stayed small and elegant but the plant itself could grow to be lanky and quite tall. The shrubs here stood nearly five feet.

Mountain willow could only grow close to the river. A microscopic tingling traveled up her neck into her mind, and everything started slowing as that drugged sensation crept back in. She fought it, but then Draven stepped closer, and the feeling intensified.

If she could just get away from him, maybe she would be able to process.

Without thinking about it, Shiloh jumped backward into the river. The frigid temperature momentarily took her breath away, and the shallow waters moved in a surprisingly swift current. She let it carry her downriver and took strong arm strokes to add momentum to her escape.

The water coursed, and her entire body submerged beneath the surface. The world slowed, and ironically, her heart rate calmed. Eyes open, she took in the smooth river rocks and the aquatic plants waving at her from below. Despite her speed, the life in the river looked stationary and wonderous.

She took what felt like an eternity, but in reality, must have only been a few seconds, to think back through Fern's natural energy lessons and Simon and Wendel's HAARP research.

Scared to lift her head but also desperately needing oxygen, she sputtered to the surface. She raised her head and scanned the banks around her. No Draven. A hanging branch outstretched its limbs as if inviting her over, and she grabbed for it. *Success.* She used it to rip herself from the speeding current and roll onto the shore, colliding with a cluster of mountain willows.

Heaving gasps shook her body, and she scrambled into the cover of the brush. She tried to calm herself and find the comfort of her tingling fingertips. She used her energy to reach out to one single leaf. It trembled and fluttered in time with her psychokinetic commands. Instead of moving to the other leaves, Shiloh let her mind grope its way down the thinnest part of the stem and into the heart of the plant. Further, she pushed until the entire shrub quivered with energy. She could sense the roots underground.

It's working.

Just like Fern had talked about. Breathing deeply, she focused all her energy on maintaining her connection and expanding it into the very tips of the plant. Initially, the knobby roots resisted, but then something clicked, like a key finally fitting into the right lock.

She held that one plant's roots in a tight cocoon and then reached for another. It also stuck. Like pieces of Play-Doh, the current began to build. Somehow, she could feel energy leaping from cell to cell, plant to plant, and soon she felt her connection growing faster than she could keep up with.

The energy of the plants took her then. An invisible force propelled her to her feet and pushed her forward, leaving her exposed for anyone to see. The forest surrounded her, but at a distance, and she knew Draven would soon spot her. Her brain told her to duck, but her body continued in a loping gate, nearly a run but not quite.

At the edge of the forest, she spotted a giant weeping willow. The tree had to be at least three feet in diameter and its luxurious branches hung over thirty feet in some places.

How? A weeping willow can't survive in this climate, especially out in the wild like this. Can it?

The tree's magnetic energy summoned her, and she ran to it. Behind her, footsteps echoed. Draven must have found her. Must have seen her.

Shit.

The tree stood only twenty or so yards away when she saw the stone at the base of its trunk. A grave marker. Not a cross, but a cement plaque of sorts. Her blood ran cold. She'd been here before.

The body. The thud. The red hair. The magnificent power of the energy storm that had followed.

The memory made her stomach roil, but it also gave her an idea. She only had one chance. If he figured out what she was going to try…

Shiloh's body slammed into the trunk, forcing her momentum to a halt. She refused to let go of her connection to the willows, though. She felt, hastily now, for the roots of the weeping willow.

Drawing him in, she felt like a cat, playing with her prey. She stood tall, shoulders squared to Draven's advancing form. Recognizing the gravesite of his mother, he slowed to a careful walk. Mariam and Margaret flanked him, and together they all moved in a careful, triangular formation.

"I see you found our tree, Shiloh. I brought you here to show you one of many worst moments of my life," Draven spoke softly.

Shiloh remained silent, singularly focused on hiding her objective.

"How dare you stand on my mother's grave?" he asked, nodding at the slab beneath Shiloh's feet, his icy tone more threatening than any physical blow he could throw.

Were they feeling this connection too? Or was her mind still singular enough that it was only her? She hoped for the latter. If Draven added the willows to his power bank…

Shiloh felt like her head might explode, the euphoric sensation ten times stronger than it had ever been before.

"Make me move," she taunted.

He paused, and Shiloh could see him considering his next move. Before he could process his options, she roared out her anger. She lifted the limbs of the massive tree, summoning the power of the connection she had crafted. Tentacle-like branched grasped empty air, and the ground shook beneath them all.

She had the tree for balance, but the tremor caught the frail Mariam and Margaret off guard and knocked them to the ground. She focused on one particularly long, draping branch. It swung and grabbed for Draven's ankles.

Her control was good but not that good.

It knocked him off his feet but failed to take hold.

Draven's anger bubbled, flushing his cheeks.

Mariam hissed like a cat.

Margaret stood motionless.

The tree hurled another one of its branches. Again and again, it punched. Shiloh tried to maintain ownership of the force of the connection but was losing control. Then just like in the sleep pod connection, all of the tree's branches rose straight into the sky. They trapped her, ready to come crashing down atop her any second.

As they swung down all at once, she ducked away from a swiftly flailing arm but not quickly enough. It smacked the back of her head so hard her vision blurred. The scab over the transmitter tore open, and thick blood gushed. Light-headedness washed over her, and she stumbled, falling to her hands and knees.

Draven's proximity worked against her now. He had regained his footing and with it his composure. *What if he gains control of the tree?* It was her only weapon. They were connected, her power now also his. The implant throbbed.

"I only come here in the dark, you know. This place. This fucking tree," Draven gestured wildly on unsteady feet. "That night, that intimate night I showed you, was when I embraced the darkness as my biggest ally."

Shiloh breathed shallowly. Crawled desperately. She needed to get to the other side of the tree. To the hollow she remembered from that horrible night.

"My mother," he paused. "She was a dumb broad, but she loved me. I didn't even have to get her high to do it."

So he does know what he's doing to Mariam.

"Why? If you know she doesn't love you, why don't you just let her go?" Shiloh rasped.

"Because almost enough is all I ever get in this life, and it's going to have to be good enough."

A high-pitched screech filled the air. The lone power line in the distance squealed like a monstrous, crying crow. It was all she could do not to cover her ears.

Mariam and Margaret fell to their knees, and Draven squinted. Mariam's body shook and seized. She foamed at the mouth like she was overdosing. At the same instant, a horrifying shock lit into the back of Shiloh's neck. A hot substance burned like a lighter from within.

"Mom!" she cried out. But between the screeching and the burning she lost her focus. Vision spotty, she fought to remain conscious. She could smell her mind cooking inside her head. Smoke wafted into her nostrils.

Then it dawned on her. It wasn't her mind burning. The smoke was real. The woods behind her were burning.

"Mariam, my love. Hold on. I know this is so much energy for your fragile heart, but you can take it," Draven encouraged, momentarily distracted.

Clasping the back of her neck, a knotted mass stuck to Shiloh's bloodied fingers and she yanked, hard. Bringing her hand back around, she peered down at the tiny node of roots. A sticky yellow substance coated some of the threadlike tips. The implant.

As suddenly as it had started, the pain stopped. She felt different, lighter. Her connection with the tree was gone but so was the woozy high. She now suspected she knew exactly what Fern planned.

This would work.

She tested, calling out to Draven's mind, but he didn't respond. Before her, he visibly sagged and crumpled, his forest burning. His power burning.

Shiloh reached out to the willow again, half expecting rejection without the help of the implant. But it welcomed her, and this time she didn't hesitate. She mustered the entire force of the willow tree and the mountain willow shrubs' energy. She ducked into the hollow chasm in the trunk of the tree a split second before the largest willow branch crashed down only yards away from Draven's feet.

The rocky dirt began to separate. As the earth quaked, it splintered. A huge piece grated away, forming a chasm at Draven's feet. Rocks, then boulders, splintered off the rapidly forming ledge, and a powerful, bottomless pit of dust swallowed them up.

Shiloh met Draven's eye for just an instant. Then the ground beneath him succumbed. Gravity ripped the once-solid earth to pieces.

He fell.

Mariam screamed, weak and anguished. Her body had stopped shaking, but she looked closer to death than life.

Shiloh's heart ached for her. Despite everything, her mother's raw distress shook her to her core.

Then Mariam started to crawl.

"*Mom!*" Shiloh screamed, running forward. The falling ground forced her back, though, and she watched, helplessly.

Mariam looked up at her, snarled, and then threw herself after Draven.

She couldn't process the senseless act; couldn't help but wonder if that jump had been Draven's final manipulation.

Margaret stood, toes over the edge of the newly formed cavern. She teetered precariously before falling backward, scrambling away from the drop.

Their eyes met, but Margaret wouldn't hold Shiloh's gaze.

Then Fern was sprinting toward them and sweeping the dazed Margaret up like a rag doll. "Move. Now," she commanded and pointed to the patch of forest near the rising smoke. "Follow me."

Shiloh, still shocked by the literal hole in the ground before her, almost didn't move out of the way fast enough.

"Come on. Now. Unless you want to end up dead."

Shiloh let her body take over once more. She couldn't allow her fear to surface, not now. They tore through the burning forest. She couldn't piece together why they were running toward the flames instead of away.

She didn't have time to question, only trust.

So she ran. Just like she had so many mornings to clear her mind. Only this time she ran for her life.

The heat from the flames singed their hair. Flying sparks made tiny holes in their clothing as they raced. The wall of fire towered around them.

Recognition dawned without warning. The narrow path before them led straight to a familiar tree. The Bendz portal. Fern's mammoth stature cleared the way for Shiloh's narrow frame. Without even hesitating, Fern dove through the impossibly small hole. It was too late to veer, so Shiloh closed her eyes and jumped, just as Fern had done—a literal leap of faith.

Shiloh landed smack on top of Fern, who let out a gruff humph. Shiloh and Margaret had to help Fern get her large body out of the narrow rock cavern's opening. Shiloh was honestly shocked Fern had fit through it the first time to follow her.

They heaved on the ground, catching their breath. Margaret sobbed and hugged Shiloh. She refused to let go. For once, Shiloh let herself be held.

"I am sorry. I am so sorry," Margaret cried, dropping her face into her hands. "I could not fight it. I should have been able to control myself, but that implant controlled me. I was like a robot. He made me kill my dear Leonard with my own two hands. And then I nearly did the same you. It was like I tried to escort you to your death in the back of a limousine. I am a murderer. Oh God."

Shiloh hugged her harder, relief flooding every fiber of her being.

CHAPTER 42

———

The darkness curled its tendrils like an octopus of fog, slowly embracing and then engulfing the light around it. The progress of death, though slow, continued, steady and unrelenting.

He gasped, breath shallow and laborious.

This was all wrong. So wrong. His underestimation would cost her.

He rolled and saw her motionless but next to him.

Mariam.

She remained loyal only to him.

Just as he always had, just as he always would, he gave in to the comforting cradle offered by the darkness.

CHAPTER 43

In the distance, weighty smoke curdled and snaked as it infiltrated the mountain skyline.

"Holy shit," Fern breathed.

"They have been right here this whole time," Margaret finished. "All these years, and they were right there." She pressed her fingertips against her closed eyes.

"Do you think…" Shiloh started, captivated by the thin grey line in the distance.

Margaret cut her off, her voice shaking. "No. They are gone."

Shiloh nodded, needing to hear someone say it out loud.

The three of them looked like they had just emerged from a war zone. Half of Fern's hair stood on end, singed. Soot streaked one dark cheek. Margaret clutched her left arm in a makeshift sling, and her face had drained of all color. Blood soaked the top of Shiloh's sweatshirt, and a twinge in her right ankle caused a slight limp. Her pupils dilated so wide that even the dim light of the setting sun caused her to squint.

Fern herded them down a narrow dirt footpath. "You both need medical attention ASAP, and you can't get it out here."

Shiloh hadn't the faintest idea of their location. That chasm that had swallowed Draven. Did she really do that? Did she kill her mother?

The fire. She hadn't done that. The events of the day felt like something that happened to a Shiloh in some other life. Not to her. Not now.

Something grabbed her arm. She screamed and jumped into the air.

Margaret screamed too. "My God, you scared the hell out of me!"

"Why did you grab me like that?" Shiloh asked.

"I want my implant removed," she stated. "I saw you get yours out, and I want you to get mine."

"Maybe we should get Arthur to do that?" Fern suggested. "We aren't exactly sterile here. Besides, yours fully latched, so it'll be harder to get. Shiloh, you're going to need a couple of stitches too probably."

Margaret opened her mouth to argue, but Fern rested a hand on her head, and Margaret thought better of it. "Fine," she said, tight lipped. "But that is the first thing we do when we get back on campus."

They moved along silently and slowly but together.

Shiloh's thoughts continued to swim. Maybe she dreamed some of it. How could so many horrible things have happened in a single day?

A horn blared, startling the birds from the surrounding trees into flight. Incredibly, Margaret's purple Mustang coupe roared into view.

"Need a ride, gals?" Wendel called from the driver's seat. Simon popped his head out the sunroof like an eager Labrador, which was almost enough to make Shiloh crack a smile. She definitely had to be hallucinating.

Margaret shook her head incredulously.

Fern waved frantically. Joyously. "It worked, guys. It really worked!"

They whooped in delight and smacked hands, momentarily looking more like teenagers than grown men.

What worked? Shiloh couldn't find a way to articulate the question aloud.

They had reached the car, but this walking path wasn't meant for sports cars. The trees stood so tightly on either side the doors could barely open.

"You cut it a little close, Fern. You had us nervous for a minute. I can't believe we did it," Simon exclaimed. "Wait a minute. Where's Mariam?"

Fern and Margaret exchanged a glance. Shiloh froze as the reality of the monstrous day hit her. It happened. All of it. It happened to her, not some far away Shiloh in another life.

"I'm so tired," she managed to muster.

Simon and Wendel's faces crumpled.

As she sank into the Mustang's backseat, Shiloh welcomed the sleep that crept up on her, unafraid for the first time in months. No nightmare could be worse than her reality.

* * *

The ambitious flames of the fireplace made Shiloh shudder when she awoke. Wendel apologetically snuffed them out and instead turned on a lamp to illuminate Fern's cozy cottage.

They'd barely made it. Somehow, they dove through the hole in the giant evergreen before it burned to the ground, but it had been much too close for comfort. Shiloh could have sworn she had sensed the swaying tree start to fall as she entered the portal.

But they made it.

Her head still throbbed, and the back of her neck stung. Her hand rose automatically to rub the pain point, and her fingers found two neat stitches.

"Do you remember Arthur coming by?" prodded Fern who had materialized from the kitchen with an oversized mug of tea.

Shiloh shook her head. She remembered falling asleep in the car but nothing else.

"He said that might happen. You were in quite a state of shock. We gave you a little something to help you sleep peacefully."

"Margaret's tracker?" she blurted shakily, still finding her words.

"All gone. Good as new," Margaret replied from the over-stuffed chair. Her arm sat in a proper sling now and a thick gauze pad covered the back of her neck. "I do not know how you pulled yours out on your own, Shiloh. It was extremely painful when Arthur detached mine. He had to sever one of my occipital nerves. The roots had attached, and it could not be saved. No long-term side effects besides some small patches of numbness on my scalp, though."

Shiloh smiled. One small piece of good news. "Fern… what happened back there?"

She smiled sadly. "Well, you executed your connection with the willow brilliantly. I'm so glad you understood why I wanted you to go to the river. You drew him in, distracted him. Then we came in for the kill." Fern winced when she realized what she had said.

Shiloh considered the sequence as she remembered it. "You mean when I lost control of the connection and the tree… You made it so powerful?"

"Yes. We finally did it. We used death as a force."

Simon jumped in. "Yeah, Fern called us, and we were able to triangulate your location. The signal kept flickering in and out, but we found it. We were able to short circuit a proximate power line. One well-placed spark and *bam*, forest fire."

"The fire spread rapidly, and because of the scale, I could finally tap into the combination of life and death forces to create an extraordinarily powerful current. Simultaneously, Draven's power faded because once the trees died, he lost their power."

"Obviously not ideal. A lot of trees had to burn before the fire got close enough for Fern to use the energy. The closest power line wasn't actually that close," Wendel explained.

"You all know I'm a pacifist and a bona fide tree-hugger, but we didn't have another option. We didn't even know if it would work," Fern added.

"What if it hadn't?" Shiloh asked.

"Plan B... not quite as elegant. I was going to tackle Draven and knock him out long enough for us to run."

Shiloh and Margaret both raised their eyebrows questioningly.

"What? I know I have a size advantage!" Fern exclaimed.

They remained silent for a long moment, thinking back. It made sense, in a twisted sort of way.

"One more thing... how did you shatter the cabin?" Shiloh asked.

"That was the simplest part of all," Fern chuckled. "I threw a big rock very hard."

Her chuckle turned into a full belly laugh, and the sound filled every crevice of the cottage. The rest of them couldn't help but join in. Even Shiloh allowed a small smile.

"You guys are truly brilliant," Shiloh acknowledged in a sad whisper.

Fern, Simon, and Wendel exchanged proud looks of accomplishment.

As they cozied up in the cottage, Shiloh swelled with mixed emotions realizing the parts each of her friends played in her fate. On the one hand, they saved her and Margaret. Without a doubt. On the other, they had all but sent her mother to her death.

She had to get out of here. She needed air. She stood up and walked onto the porch, away from the quiet conversation of the cottage.

Her breathing picked up speed. The harder she tried to suck in air, the less she actually got. A drowning sensation took over her lungs. Her mom's face swam in her memories. Her poor, wretched, beautiful mother. Gone... again. Snuffed out of Shiloh's life, and the world. Again. It didn't hurt any less this time around. In fact, the heartbreak she had been experiencing most of her life paled in comparison to the hollowed-out feeling suffocating her now.

How could she miss someone she didn't even know?

This time, though, only Shiloh would miss her. Her father hadn't even known Mariam was alive.

Breathe. Breathe. She couldn't. It was too much. Her world spun, and her limbs shook like autumn leaves.

Then she felt a bony hand on her shoulder. Margaret smiled down at her, a sad, knowing smile. She sat on the stoop next to Shiloh and curled her legs into her chest.

"Do not forget. I loved her too. I miss her too. If it is okay, I would like to mourn her with you. Or rather, remember her with you."

Shiloh's deep brown eyes flicked to Margaret, and she leaned in, falling into a clumsy half-hug.

"How could she choose him over us?"

Margaret sighed. "Unfortunately, that is a question I doubt we will ever have an answer to. We know she was not herself anymore. Maybe she jumped. Maybe he manipulated her. Either way, she cemented her fate. You or Fern or I, we could not have done anything more."

The practical part of Shiloh's brain knew this, but her heart couldn't accept it. Not yet.

"We loved her. We knew her. As she lived before. And as she died when she left us this time," Margaret continued. Her words stung, but her tone soothed Shiloh's anxiety like a lullaby. "She was great, but more importantly, she was loved. That is what matters. We loved her. You. Me. Fern. The Revned community. Even your father. She. Was. Loved."

Shiloh sighed. How did Margaret always seem to know exactly what to say? For once she didn't feel the need to explain herself or justify her emotions.

That was how it would be different this time. It still hurt. It still burned. The emptiness of loss would still threaten to overpower her some days. But this time she had others to help carry the burden of grief. Others to trust. When it felt unbearable, instead of burying herself, she could lean in, and Margaret would catch her. Her family—not the one she was born into but the one who had opened their doors and their arms to her when she had literally no one else—would be there to lend her their strength.

She had never been more at home.

ACKNOWLEDGMENTS

Thank you to my early supporters, the people who have believed in me and cheered me on from the start of this dream. I couldn't have done it with you.

Abby Farrell
Abby Lechner
Alethea Paradis
Alex Peek
Alexander Kendl
Alissa Leung
Allison Howard
Aly Spencer
Alyssa Curci
Amy Lewis
Amy Osborne
Andre Gombas
Angela Sinkler
Ani Ermoyan
Anna Dille
Anne Frisz
Anthony Rubino

Ashley Nanayakkara
Ashley Vollaro
Babette Hohrath
Barbara Rubino
Brittany Gonzalez
Camille Smith
Candace Smith
Carly Coons
Carly Deskins
Chad Brisendine
Chelsea Modesto
Chris Paradis
Christine Gravelle
Christine Gurdon
Cindy Gomez
Clarissa Picone
Colleen Itzen

Colleen Olson
Cristina Downey
Dana Hall
Daniel Hudson
Danielle Olson
Darci Liley
Darla Courtney
Dawn Rubino
Destini Simmons
Devon Jensen
Diane Murphy
Donna Kalbfleisch
E. Page Cunningham
Ellesse DesMarteau
Emily Garnier
Eric Koester
Eric Taylor
Erin Harmon
Erin Walter
Esperanza Woodman
    Navarro
Evelyn Paradis
Fran Eastman
Fred Thomas
Gina McReynolds
Gina Rembert
Gregg Smith
Gregory Klepeis
Harley Abrams
Heather Omsberg
Heidi Baskfield
Imevbore Ojebuoboh

Iris Cintron
Janet Schwenn
Jason Williams
Jeff Garnier
Jeffrey Meehan
Jeffrey Smith
Jennifer Draklellis
Jennifer A. Coggin
Jenny Bissonnette
Jeremy Rosenthal
John Bolich
John Schultz
Josh Griffin
Judy Hofflund
Julia Oleksiak
Julianne Koch
Julie Ammary
Karen Ferrie
Karen Olson
Kathy Bernal
Katie Dake
Katie Denman
Katie Phillips
Kayla Larson
Keith Brotzman
Kelly Burke
Keri Schreckengost
Kerry Rounds
Kerry Seeger
Kevin Olson
Kimmy Martinsky
Kristin Vickrey

Kuljeet Rai
Liz Stewart
Lorraine Smith
Malorie DeStefano
Mark Heston
Mary Albers
Mary Caitlin Heintzelman
Matt Gebhardt
Matt Griffiths
Melissa Feeney
Michele Dunbar
Morgan Thomas
Morgan Wager
Nikki Wiederaenders
O'Re Berry
Paul Paradis
Philippe Paradis
Priscilla Barletta
Rachel Frisz
Rebecca Paranto
Richard Smith
Rob Herb
Roger Arndt
Ron Johns
Sammie Jones
Scott Frieling
Sean Foley
Sharon Kirby
Stacey Coss
Summer Elliot
Susan Dick
Susan Goldenstein
Sydney Bornstein
Tara Jablonski
Taylor Shields
Taylor Wise
Tim Brennan
Tracy Riter
Trena Berube
Trevor Fisher
Vickie Adams
Wendy Campbell
Wendy Fong
Wendy Mendenhall

A special thank you to my beta readers for their early support and for looking in my blind spots to help bring this story to life.

Bailey Massey
Brandy Dale
Courtney Patterson
David Epp
Erin Hinton
Erin Willis
Gigi Paradis
Joann Pilkington
Katie Byrd
Liz Lucas

Matt Mutarelli
Michael Balzano
Nicole Provenza
Noel Morrill

Rebekah McIntyre
Sandra Weaver
Susan Anglin

APPENDIX

AUTHOR'S NOTE:

Boyd, Robynne. 2008. "Do People Only Use 10 Percent of Their Brains?" *Scientific American,* February 7, 2008. https://www.scientificamerican.com/article/do-people-only-use-10-percent-of-their-brains/.

Rio Times Staff. 2022. "Knowledge Transfer from Brain-To-Brain and Remote Control of the Human Body and Mind Is Already Reality." *The Rio Times.* January 17, 2022.https://www.riotimesonline.com/brazil-news/modern-day-censorship/knowledge-transfer-from-brain-to-brain-and-remote-control-of-the-human-body-and-mind-is-already-reality/.

Wohlleben, Peter. 2021. *The Heartbeat of Trees: Embracing Our Ancient Bond with Forests and Nature.* Vancouver: Greystone Books.